HI CACTI

In loving memory of my Nanny Joy

First published in 2021 by Leaping Hare Press
an imprint of The Quarto Group.
The Old Brewery, 6 Blundell Street
London, N7 9BH,
United Kingdom
T (0)20 7700 6700
www.QuartoKnows.com

A catalogue record for this book is available from the British Library.

ISBN 978-0-7112-6175-4
Ebook ISBN 978-0-7112-6176-1

10 9 8 7 6 5 4 3 2 1

Commissioning editor Monica Perdoni
Cover and interior illustrations by Maya Doyle
Design by Emily Portnoi
Edited by Caroline Earle
Photographs © Xavier Buendia: 114, 124; © Emma Croman: 4, 17, 131; © Maya Doyle: 138; © Heath Herring: 110; © Dan Ladd: 4, 7, 18, 22, 28, 32, 36, 40, 42, 52, 57, 127; © Adrienne Leonard on Unsplash: 44; © Kenny McCracken: 4, 8, 11, 13, 19, 21, 24, 25, 30, 31, 33, 35, 37-39, 41, 46-49, 51, 53-55, 58-67, 71, 72, 75, 78-89, 102, 104, 107, 111, 112, 116-122, 125, 128, 129, 132; © Sabina Palermo: 4, 20, 26, 27, 43, 50, 68, 76, 92-101, 103, 105, 109, 123, 130, 132-134, 137, 139, 141; © Shutterstock: 74 (Tatiana Dyuvbanova), 103 (images72), 117 (JulianJD); © Fiona Thomson: 136.

Printed in China

HI CACTI

Growing Houseplants & Happiness

Sabina Palermo

CONTENTS

INTRODUCTION

Hi y'all, I'm Sabina, founder of the colourful botanical business Hi Cacti. I'm here to preach the joys and benefits that cultivating, nurturing and caring for houseplants can have on your happiness and wellbeing. Some call me 'the girl next door of easy-care houseplants' and others call me the 'crazy cactus lady', but as long as you call me, right?

THE JOURNEY

Throughout this book I also want to share some of the places, faces and experiences that helped spur me on my path to creating Hi Cacti. My business started with a sinking feeling that I was failing at adulthood when I even struggled to just keep my houseplants alive, and then life's random experiences led me back to my roots, which inspired me to blaze this new trail. This journey didn't just turn me from a 'plant killer' to an enthusiast, but helped me grow into a botanical entrepreneur as well.

I want to level with you – I'm not a botanist and I didn't go to horticulture school. I'm not writing this book as a scientist or a doctor – any 'expertise' has been self-taught by my trials and triumphs along the way. I've built my botanical business from scratch on my own with no business degree. Heck, when I started on this Hi Cacti journey in 2015 my business was called Prick Cactus and it was a pleasure project. I was thrilled to bits when people were even slightly interested in what I was doing, albeit most of my friends and family thought my idea of a cactus shop

was kind of crazy and very niche. The whole point was to help others who, like me at the time; were not gifted with 'green fingers', so I started hand-making colourful concrete pots and pairing them with low-maintenance cacti and succulents. Once my confidence with other easy-care indoor houseplants started to grow, my business also literally grew from there!

PLANT POSITIVITY

I realized early on the impact of adding these new plant babies into my home, it gave me a new level of fulfilment, peace, comfort and love of my space and made me feel more at home and calm. Over the last five years of running my business, I've seen first hand the positivity that occurs when we coexist with houseplants. Customers' faces light up when they are passing by my botanical boutique and see the greenery and plant life pouring out on to the path. I see how people stop in their tracks for a moment to appreciate the beauty and aesthetic of plants – they really do make us feel good. People are drawn to the greenery and touch the foliage; it's really pretty magical to

watch how strangers stop, smile and enjoy this natural engagement with the simple company of plants.

Through this book I want to share the ways in which plants help enrich our physical, mental and spiritual wellbeing. I will share recommendations for some of my favourite easy-care houseplants to enable you to create your own low-maintenance jungle indoors. And a few crafty DIYs, tips and recipes to make it easy, fun and inspiring to add some feel-good greenery into our daily lives.

PLANTS WEREN'T ALWAYS MY BAG

Let's rewind to about six years ago, before I started Hi Cacti and before I had any houseplants in my life. I was in a job that didn't fulfil me. I was always busy. I rented a small, damp flat in the English seaside city of Brighton, where cost of living is high and you are lucky if you have an outdoor space. I was

about to turn thirty and owned nothing; I wasn't allowed a pet and didn't feel even close to having kids. I was worried that all these things combined with my long-term boyfriend and I still being unmarried, somehow meant that my life didn't fit into the picture I had imagined. Then my role model and idol died: my grandmother, Nanny Joy. Devastated and mourning while helping my mother and grandad clear her belongings, I inherited her small cactus collection and a handmade pendant with a desert landscape that she used to wear, which is one of my most prized treasures.

That's how this story started – a displaced, thirtysomething gal from Austin, Texas, desperately attempting to keep her grandmother's memory alive through her inherited cacti in not-so-sunny England. Little did I know that me and these cacti would grow together into a new hobby that would turn into a fresh career path – Nanny Joy would have loved this story.

'BLOOM WHERE YOU'RE PLANTED'

PLANT CARE AS SELF-CARE

Instead of the typical books on plants that can be a sterile 'how to' or plant encyclopedia, I want to create an alternative botanical empowerment guide – a book that shares and captures the 'feel-good' qualities and beauty that houseplants bring us. Through my business and this book I celebrate plant care as a form of self-care, and the everyday ways in which to bring the outdoors in. In this digital age where we are often overwhelmed, we can find some inspiration to reconnect and be rooted to nature in small ways. And I will let you in on a little secret – it's good for you! Your mind, body and spirit can all be enriched by these magical green botanical things that grow in the cracks of the pavements, gardens, the kitchen, the park, the forest ... okay you get my drift.

From epic adventures of exploring the great natural outdoors to small and simple interactions with houseplants, nature affects us in a multitude of ways.

BLOOM WHERE YOU'RE PLANTED

'Bloom where you're planted' is a mantra that struck me and left an impression from my road trips around the southwest of America, but more specifically from Tucson, Arizona. Tucson, where I was fuelled by epic drives, tacos and cactus desert hikes followed by margaritas, felt like a second home. My boyfriend Dan and I were road tripping from LA to Austin and were only really passing through Tucson to break up our route, but we fell so hard for it we changed our itinerary to extend our stay. We saw this motto of 'Bloom where you're planted' pop up across the city and the desert in various forms: bumper stickers, street art, T-shirts, and even on beer coolers. When you're in that part of the world, you understand why this mindful quote hits home with the locals as a tiding of perseverance and hope – sometimes in life it feels tough to survive, let alone bloom, when you find yourself in the desert.

NATURE'S LIFE LESSONS

The mind-blowing contrast of travelling from the lush greenery of England to the heat of the Arizona desert, and then to witness plants and flowers rising up from the red clay and rocky earth is awe-inspiring. Thousands of giant saguaro cacti hold their heads up to 12 metres (40 feet) high, and despite the heat and lack of rain they still thrive. Nature and her plants provide mindful daily lessons, from finding motivation in how a dropped seed has become a tree within the confinements of blocks of paved concrete, to literally taking pleasure in 'the fruits of your labour' by picking a tomato off the vine that you planted. You don't have to dig deep to reconnect to nature to enjoy its simple pleasures and motivational moments, just occasionally slow down and take the time to 'smell the roses'. Breathe in deeply and reflect on the abundance that nature shares with us. Surrounding yourself with plants brings life and a breath of fresh air to your space.

THE BENEFITS

Our ancient ancestors worshipped plants and celebrated nature – they basked in her glories and utilized her plants for shelter, nourishment and to survive. Since then, we've exchanged our lives in the forests for city life and we are beginning to see the negative effects and the void that this distance from nature is creating within us. Time for a botanical feel-good intervention!

RECONNECTING TO NATURE CAN BE SIMPLE

Mindfully adding more nature and plant life to everyday living, even small additions like walking down a leafy street, relaxing in a garden or nurturing an indoor plant can benefit your wellbeing and health in more ways than you think. Nowadays, even though we spend most of our time indoors (an estimated 93 per cent of the time on average for Americans and 90 per cent for Europeans), science shows that our brains still crave the green outdoors, so much so that even seeing the colour green relaxes and calms our busy brains. When us city dwellers aren't able to get outdoors into nature easily or frequently, we still benefit from those same calming and reviving effects by greening up our homes, workspaces or urban spaces.

JUST WHAT THE DOCTOR ORDERED

Plants can act as a green tonic by making us feel welcome and more relaxed in a space or environment.

Numerous studies have also shown that simply adding plants and flowers to a hospital room had positive effects on patients' recovery. Plants and trees release a chemical called phytoncide, which has been found to boost our immune systems, so we aren't the only ones prescribing some greenery in your life – doctors in Scotland are prescribing 'nature' in the first initiative of its kind in the UK, but I believe others will begin to follow this green medicine worldwide. Studies show that spending time in nature reduces stress, anxiety and depression while boosting your immune system, reducing blood pressure, aiding sleep and improving concentration and memory. Plants also boost concentration, so offices and schools can benefit from these botanical-based focusing tools.

PLANTS (REALLY DO) MAKE US HAPPY

It's easy to lose sight of the fact that we come from the natural world, so turning to nature for cures for our ailments or for peace and comfort is, well, natural really. Throughout these pages I invite you to reflect on your everyday life and think about the presence of plants and the natural world around you. Give yourself a simple grounding by taking just a few minutes each day to consciously soak up a mindful moment in nature. This can be done simply in a garden, a park, by taking a brief walk or even tending to or touching some of the plants in your home or office. You might even be lucky enough to have access to some beautiful nature on your doorstep, so I challenge you to try and have a moment catching up with your mama – Mother Nature that is – in whatever capacity that you are able to or desire.

NATURE BASKING

Give yourself this dedicated time either daily, or even just weekly, to consciously soak up some 'you time' and just be present in nature – let's call it a mindful 'nature basking'. How do you feel when you sit in a garden, look up at trees, take off your shoes to feel the grass or earth under your feet, or feel the sky's expanse above you? Calm? Grounded? Relaxed? Connected? Still? Try even in a small way to experience and feel nature that isn't behind a pane of glass or on a screen. You can alter these prompts to suit your setting or terrain, and in time think of your own prompts to bask in from your natural setting.

Now you can start to grasp why I feel so passionate about this book and my mission for my business Hi Cacti: to encourage accessible ways to bring greenery into our daily, busy and predominantly indoor lives to benefit our overall wellbeing.

PLANT THERAPY

In my plant shop I have been blown away by the increase in customers, of all ages, telling me that their therapist and/or doctor have prescribed getting an indoor plant to help their depression, grief, anxiety or addiction.

Alongside modern medicine and in our technological age, it warms my heart to hear that we are beginning to come full circle in our appreciation and understanding of the multitude of benefits that nature and her plant life can bring us. The act of caring and being responsible for a plant and watching it grow and bloom gives a sense of purpose and accomplishment, which can be so healing and comforting alongside therapy.

CHAPTER 1

EASY-CARE HOUSE-PLANTS

These are my personal faves and recommendations for beautiful and low-maintenance indoor plants for beginners or green-fingered pros alike – all welcome!

SNOWFLAKE ALOE

LET'S GET STARTED

SOME NEED-TO-KNOWS BEFORE YOU BEGIN

Guys, I first need to level with you about books, magazines and blogs telling you that certain plants are un-killable or 'best' for certain rooms or spaces like a bathroom or an office. You are clever and logical, so I'm sure you can guess that plants are not immortal and even the easiest plants still need some care occasionally. I've also heard customers say things like, 'Well plants just grow, right?' True, they can, but if you take an exotic plant that grows wild in the dry sunny heat of southern Africa and rehome it indoors in your low-light apartment in Seattle, it will need the right spot and care to acclimatize to its new adoptive life in the city. Suggestions for plants that suit a west-facing window or for 'bathroom-happy' plants can help shed some insight into their desired environment, but it's still best to look at a plant's origin in nature and all its needs before selecting the best spot. Take a Cheese Plant, for example, which likes bright filtered light, then you read a blog suggesting that a bathroom is a good spot because the plant likes moist humid air. However, your bathroom window may be frosted and the lighting low, so you end up with a sad, light-hungry Cheese Plant because the blogger based this recommendation on the plant's air preference and not its lighting needs.

LET THERE BE LIGHT

Everyone's home or workspace has varying light and temperatures that can affect a plant's needs. Paying a little bit of attention to your space's lighting first can help you select plants to play to your space's strengths. As well as keeping your plants happy, this can save you time, energy and money when trying to green up your space. For this reason, I decided to group my favourite plants according to lighting needs because this is the first question I ask my customers when helping them to pick perfect and happy plants for their needs and space.

A few thoughts worth mentioning before we journey together through my top houseplant list. First, when we talk about plants' lighting needs, we are talking about natural light from the sun, not artificial indoor light from bulbs. So if I recommend a plant that's good for a bright space and you want plants for your office workspace, which is full of artificial lights, maybe go in before or after work or switch off all the lights to check out the strength of the natural lighting before selecting plants (see page 86 for my artificial light hack).

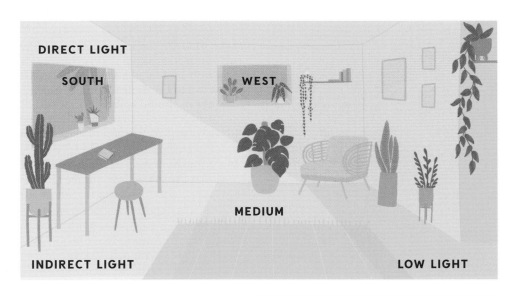

DIRECT LIGHT

SOUTH

WEST

MEDIUM

INDIRECT LIGHT

LOW LIGHT

OUR LIGHTING CATEGORIES:

- **Sunny and Bright** – this category likes bright light to full sun, without light obstruction from blinds, trees, signs or buildings.
- **Bright and Filtered** – prefers no direct sun and sunlight should be diffused or dappled by curtains, blinds, trees or other obstructions.
- **Low Light-Tolerant** – prefers no direct sun and a shady spot.
- **Flexible** – the hint is in the name and this category is for plants with versatile lighting needs.

FIND YOUR LIGHT

A little trick if you need help gauging lighting in a room is to hold your hand around 30cm (1ft) over a piece of white printing paper:
- If you see a clear and sharp shadow – Bright Light
- Your hand creates a fuzzy shadow – Filtered Light
- You only see a blob – Low Light

SURVIVING VS. THRIVING

When I discuss my recommendations for care, this is to give plants their ideal needs to thrive, but many of the plants I'm highlighting are pretty hardcore and tolerant. You might find a cactus, for example, can 'survive' for quite a while without my recommendation of some direct sunlight, but it won't necessarily show signs of thriving, such as growth or blossoming. We are similar with our surviving versus thriving. For each of us, the ideal amount of sunlight, air, water and food we need to survive versus the ideal amount to thrive are two different things, but we are slightly more complicated cucumbers than that!

'Less light' means water less, so whether your plant is in a low-lit spot or it's winter, your soil will retain more moisture compared to plants receiving more light or heat in the warmer months. Either water less often and/or give them less to drink each time.

A POT TO CALL HOME

Most houseplants need water to be able to flow or escape through them so the plant doesn't sit in water – this can lead to root rot and therefore a pot with good drainage can be key into a plant's health. We will discuss pot, drainage and more watering tips on pages 70–73.

BYE–BYE INDOOR AIR POLLUTION

This incredible green gift that plants give will be discussed throughout this book. But even when I highlight specific plants for their amazing air-purifying benefits, I must emphasize that having any houseplants will purify indoor air by releasing fresh oxygen. However, some plant species have a greater capacity for removing air toxins called VOCs (volatile organic compounds) than other plants. According to Dr. Bill Wolverton from NASA, it's good to have at least two plants per 9.3 square metres (100 square feet), so the more the merrier.

Bacteria and viruses can hitch rides on dust particles, but indoor plants can counteract this as they are particle cleaners in your home. There have been numerous studies carried out, testing the effectiveness of specific plants for removing VOCs. Examples of these indoor toxins can be found in a variety of materials – paints, wood varnishes, detergents, floor finishes, carpets and other soft furnishings. These, combined with diminished airflow in a home, can make indoor air pollution a real issue. These synthetic building materials and new furnishing toxins make up 90 per cent of all indoor air pollution. A study has shown that the inside of your home can be more polluted than the outdoor air in a major industrial city.

boosting oxygen than others. These are usually plants with many leaves or large, broad leaves.

VARIETY IS THE SPICE OF LIFE

My top plant list couldn't fit everything in that I would have liked, but the care and needs of many of the plants discussed are the same for related plants. So, for example, my tips on the Candelabra Aloe can be used for other types of Aloes, tips on the Prickly Pear Cactus can be used for caring for other cacti, and the Cheese Plant is the same for the Monkey Mask Monstera and so forth.

INDOORS VERSUS OUTDOORS

Many of these plants can grow outdoors if your climate is similar to their native terrains. So, all my care instructions are based on treatment of these plants for indoor use, but if you want any of these for outdoor use as well just double-check their Hardiness Zones to make sure that they are suitable for your climate.

BREATH OF FRESH AIR

Another benefit houseplants bring to our indoor air is the boost of oxygen. Plants and us are a match made in heaven. All plants release oxygen and breathe in carbon dioxide through different forms of photosynthesis, giving us oxygen to breathe and in return we release carbon dioxide for plants – this is cohabiting chemistry at its best! Some indoor plants have greater capacities for producing

POTHOS

Epipremnum aureum

AKA:

Devil's Ivy, Ivy Arum, Golden Pothos, Ceylon Creeper, Hunter's Robe, Money Plant.

These are very popular indoor plants for a reason. The leafy and beautiful Pothos are great for beginners or for workspaces as they are adaptable and easy to tend to – they can handle erratic watering, tolerate low light and are fast growing.

These evergreens are usually seen growing well in a hanging planter or up along a moss pole. Pothos are also easy to propagate (see pages 80–85). Plants in this genus come in a few leaf variations such as Marble Queen or Neon Pothos (another fave,) and commonly get confused with the similar-looking plant Heartleaf Philodendron – see page 87 to tell the difference.

HOME GROWN

Originally from the Solomon Islands – it can grow wild up to 20m (66ft) in forest canopies and along tree trunks in Polynesia and Southeast Asia.

SUN

Prefers filtered or dappled light to moderate shade as the leaves can burn in sun. Low light-tolerant, so can survive poor light conditions.

AIR

Likes moderate humidity.

WATER

Water thoroughly about once a week, but allow the soil to dry out between waterings – do the 'touch test' to feel the top 5cm (2in) of soil. The leaves will wilt to hint that it's thirsty and then 'ping' back to normal as they hydrate.

GROWING TOGETHER

Ancient Chinese feng shui encourages planting Pothos in your surroundings to promote good luck and bring good fortune. The practice of feng shui uses energy forces to harmonize and balance people with their surrounding environment, and one way that this is promoted is through adding certain plant life into your spaces. It's amazing how for centuries so many cultures all over the world have been making the connections to humanity's happiness and harmony through adding plant life.

SHE'S NO DEVIL

Don't worry, this plant's nickname 'Devil's Ivy' isn't referencing bad voodoo or anything menacing! These shady plants grow wild in dark crevices of forests, hence being a 'friend to darkness'.

PEACE LILY

Spathiphyllum varieties

AKA:

White Sails.

The Peace Lily literally grows fresh air. Despite her name she ain't a lily, this goddess-like plant is one of the highest-ranking plants for air purification as it removes volatile organic compounds, such as solvents, from the air and cleanses away airborne moulds, which can help those with asthma and allergies. To top that she showcases her elegant white hooded flowers almost all year round.

If your Peace Lily's leaves droop, she needs a drink – drama queen really tells you when she's thirsty. This magical plant also regulates moisture and humidity levels in a room, making the air balanced to breathe with ease, which is ideal for aiding sleep and relaxation – and great if you have a space with a damp issue.

 HOME GROWN

Native to Venezuela, Colombia and other tropical rainforests in the Americas.

SUN

Prefers filtered or dappled light to partial shade as the leaves burn in direct sun. Low light-tolerant, so can survive poor light conditions.

 AIR

Likes moderate humidity.

 WATER

Water thoroughly about once a week. The soil wants to be kept slightly moist, but not wet. The leaves droop to signal they need water and then 'ping' back to normal the next day as they hydrate.

EASY-CARE HOUSEPLANTS

GROWING TOGETHER

Peace Lilies go through a process called 'transpiration', in which they release moisturizing vapour from their roots into the air from the underside canopy of their leaves. Interesting factoid there, but why so helpful? Well, a new study reveals that adding plants such as Peace Lilies to your space can help moisturize your skin. There you were trying to find an affordable and all-natural moisturizer when a pretty leafy pal that sits prettier on the shelf can help! Horticultural scientist

Tijana Blanusa conducted a study that revealed how plants with high transpiration rates and large leaf canopies, especially Peace Lilies and ivy varieties, show results in hydrating human skin. They can also counteract the effects of air caused by climate, lack of ventilation or heaters. The study also showed that multiple plants can help increase the moisturizing effects, so the more the merrier – good news for those of us trying to justify our growing plant collection!

HEART-LEAF PHILODENDRON

Philodendron scandens

AKA:
Sweetheart Plant.

Heart-leaf Philodendrons create a luscious, cascading jungle with ease. Variety is the spice of life and the Philodendron genus have 480 species ranging in shapes, sizes and colours. Many climb or trail, but some Philodendrons varieties grow upwards, but care remains similar. The heart-leafs are renowned for their easy care, speedy growth and beautiful heart leaves. Also ideal for propagating to create more baby sweethearts, so check out how on pages 80–85. My favourite varieties are scandens 'Brasil' with bright lemon and lime pointed heart shaped leaves and 'Micans' with dark green velvet hearts with dusty pink under leaf.

HOME GROWN

Can be found hanging out on large tree trunks in tropical forests in the Americas and the Caribbean at natural lengths of 6m (20ft) long.

SUN

Prefers filtered or dappled light to moderate shade as the leaves can yellow and burn in sun.

AIR

Likes moderate humidity, so thrives with misting or in humid spaces such as kitchens or bathrooms.

WATER

From spring to autumn water thoroughly once a week. Prefers to be kept slightly moist but allow the top 2.5cm (1in) of soil to dry to the touch before watering. In the winter months allow the soil to dry out between waterings.

GROWING TOGETHER

Along the vines where new leaves have formed you can find a thin brown papery trace from which the new leaf stemmed. This is the remnant of a temporary protective sheath that the plant forms to shield baby leaves while they are weak and forming. Once the leaf is strong enough and starts to cast out, this sheath's work is done, so it dries up quickly. These will eventually drop off, but when we touch the plant and carefully remove these wilted papers it doesn't just help keep our plant looking good, it helps retain its energy for new growth and life. This little mindful act is also a relaxing moment in which to engage with nature and give yourself a boost. Take a moment to reflect that you owe the new heart-shaped leaves on your Philodendron to those sheaths. Now when you see these little brown traces you will know it's a good sign – a happy, healthy plant is growing.

CHINESE EVERGREENS
Aglaonema varieties

FAVES:
Silver Queen,
Red Aglaonema.

Chinese Evergreens are small, slow-growing, shade-loving, happy-go-lucky plants. They are known for their easy care, decorative patterns and beautifully marbled foliage. Aglaonemas are ancient plants that have been kept as decorative and lucky plants in Asia for centuries. Their crown of elongated oval leaves comes in an array of colours from silvers and greens to pinks, reds and creams – the darker varieties are able to withstand lower light conditions and those with brighter colours will retain their brilliance if given more filtered light. They are flexible characters and tolerant of inconsistent carers, so can forgive sporadic watering and be flexible with lighting, which makes this plant a great pal for busy bees or out-of-towners.

 HOME GROWN

Native to tropical and subtropical under-forest canopies in Asia and New Guinea.

 SUN

Prefers filtered medium indirect light to moderate shade. They are low light-tolerant and don't like direct sun.

AIR

Likes moderate humidity but keep it away from draughts; enjoys a warm misting occasionally.

 WATER

Water thoroughly every week or two, but 'touch test' to feel the top 5cm (2in) to allow the soil to dry out between waterings. Decrease waterings in winter or when light levels are low.

GROWING TOGETHER

Chinese Evergreens also top 'green helper' lists. They are powerful air-purifying plant that release fresh oxygen throughout the day and clears the air of harmful industrial and day-to-day pollutants such as formaldehyde. Formaldehyde? Never heard of it? But you are surrounded by it. Formaldehyde can be found outdoors in car fumes and indoors in tobacco, new products and new constructions. It can also be found in manufactured wood products such as flooring, cabinets and furniture as well as in fabrics used for curtains or soft furnishings. Also, certain household products such as glues, coatings, paints, disinfectants, pesticides and cosmetics can contain formaldehyde. So, to help eliminate some of these nasty carcinogens, you can add these green housemates to help household health.

DUMB CANE

Dieffenbachia seguine

AKA:

Tropic Snow, Leopard Lily, Mother-in-Law's Tongue.

If you like big leaves, and ya cannot lie, then a difficult-to-say *Dieffenbachia* is for you. This impressive houseplant is a show-stopper with beautifully large ornate leaves that are spotted and decoratively marked like a snow leopard – hence the references in some of the nicknames for this bold beauty. The more common nickname Dumb Cane derives from the mildly poisonous liquid that can drip from its leaves, which contains raphides that can leave your tongue feeling temporarily 'dumb' or numb if ingested, but symptoms are mild in pets and humans.

She was tested in a NASA study and found to remove formaldehyde, xylene and toluene VOCs (volatile organic compounds) from the air, so this lady is another powerful air purifier.

HOME GROWN

Native to tropical forests of Central and South America from Mexico down to south Argentina.

SUN

Prefers filtered medium indirect light to partial shade. They are low light-tolerant and the leaves burn in direct sun.

AIR

Loves humidity so wipe the leaves occasionally with a moist towel or mist if kept in a dry space.

WATER

Water thoroughly every week but let the soil dry out between waterings – 'touch test' to feel the top 5cm (2in). Decrease waterings in winter.

TADPOLE CRIBS

In Costa Rica, researchers found that the increase or decrease of the population of colourful poison dart frogs in the rainforests correlated heavily to the abundance of Dumb Cane. These frogs lay almost all of their tadpoles on Dumb Cane leaves.

GROWING TOGETHER

As this is a tropical queen of a plant she also absorbs damp and humidity (plus nasty airborne moulds) from a space or room – this can help those who struggle with respiratory issues to breathe clearly. My partner is asthmatic and our bedroom is susceptible to damp, so we have one in the room to help suck the moisture from the air and keep his chest clear at night – then we both get a good night's sleep.

RECLAIM YOUR WILD.

COWBOY CACTUS

Euphorbia ingens

AKA:

Candelabra Tree,
Cactus Spurge,
Milk Tree.

Oh, hey there, cowboy! This is a tall, handsome and structural cacti, well, technically it's a succulent, but because of its iconic 'cactus' shape and large spikes it is commonly referred to as a cactus. *Euphorbia* is one of the largest genus of plants – with over 2,000 species, and about 1,200 of them are succulents.

Be mindful as these cowboys can bite back – they have developed a defence mechanism against animal predators – a milky sap inside, which is mildly toxic and can cause slight irritation to the skin or mouth if ingested. Cowboy Cacti can be used in outdoor landscaping in warmer climates, but for many it's best to keep them primarily indoors as they prefer dry conditions and won't tolerate frost.

 HOME GROWN

Native to southern parts of Africa.

 SUN

Likes bright natural light and thrives in 4–6 hours of direct sun a day, but can still survive without direct sun in a bright spot.

 AIR

Likes dry to low humidity.

 WATER

A good rule of thumb is once a month. In warmer periods every two weeks, but touch test that the soil is bone dry before watering. Use a spray bottle to wet the soil around the base of the cactus to prevent overwatering. During late autumn to early spring, water once every couple of months as this is their dormant period.

SETTING THE RECORD STRAIGHT: CACTUS VS. SUCCULENT

A lot of people think if it has spikes or 'pricks' then it's a cactus, or if it has fleshy 'fat leaves' like our friend the Aloe then it's a succulent. Ain't wrong, but a common misconception! The long and short of it is all cacti are succulents, but not all succulents are cacti, if you get me. Cacti are from a single botanical family, while 'succulent' is a looser term and a number of botanical families contain a few different types of succulent.

GROWING TOGETHER

Save water and buy a cactus. Cacti are an ethical choice of houseplant when you think about their sustainability. They have long life spans and of course are drought-tolerant so require very little water – they can go months without water or on very little moisture. So, whether you live in a terrain where you have water shortages or not, bear in mind that the more resources you use, the more will need to be replenished from our planet's resources. Picture cacti as resilient little eco warriors!

CANDELABRA ALOE

Aloe arborescens

AKA:
*Torch Aloe,
Krantz Aloe.*

These bluey-green gel-based pals are a staple in many households, but Aloes are ancient plants whose magical qualities have been harnessed medicinally and spiritually for thousands of years.

Aloe vera is a powerful and useful plant, but my personal preference is for the Candelabra Aloe. It is prettier, perkier and a more pleasing shape, while Aloe vera can grow with big heavy leaves that tend to droop. It also has higher levels of medicinal properties. The smaller leaves are a better size for individual uses – Aloe vera can look like it's lost a limb when you take a cutting, while the Candelabra Aloe has lots of smaller leaves so it's not as noticeable.

HOME GROWN

Native to the Arabian Peninsula, southern Africa, Madagascar and Jordan. They now grow wild around the world from Mexico to China.

SUN

Enjoys a sunny spot and can tolerate some direct sun, but prefers bright filtered light as it can scorch in too much strong direct sun.

AIR

Likes dry to low humidity.

WATER

A good rule of thumb is once a month. In hotter periods every two weeks, but touch test to check the soil is bone dry before watering. Spray soil at the base to wet but not saturate it. It is dormant late autumn to early spring so water less, roughly once every couple of months.

GROWING TOGETHER

This super-practical plant makes a handy housemate so can be a thoughtful gift as a household essential for many reasons. Aloes are known to be soothing and healing for rashes, dry skin, bites, itches, scratches, burn, and scars. To top it off, one pot of Aloe is equal to nine biological air cleaners – they're notable for cleaning toxins from the air and removing benzene and formaldehyde, by-products of chemical-based cleaners, varnishes, detergents and paints.

This makes it the perfect housewarming gift to help absorb those nasty 'new home' toxins. Aloes are also renowned for how easily they grow 'pups' (see page 84)making this a friendly and easy way to share the love from your mama Aloe – give a baby pup as a little 'hello' to an elderly neighbour or new colleague, or as a thank-you or thinking-of-you gift. Think of all the homes a 'pay it forward' Aloe could bring a li'l sunshine to, let alone all the smooth skin and clean air!

ZEBRA HAWORTHIA

Haworthia fasciata

AKA:

Zebra Plant, Haworthia 'Big Band', Zebra Cactus, Zebra Aloe.

These sculptural and hardy evergreens are succulents that usually grow with swirling layers of thick, firm leaves in a rosette shape. They are easy-peasy, eye-catching and grow in firm and compact sizes, so they are great for smaller spaces . They are often confused with Aloes due to their look and shape, but are smaller and flower into a more distinct bell shape, usually white, instead of the torch-like shoots of a flowering Aloe. There are about 70 different species of *Haworthia* but I'm highlighting the Zebra Haworthia as it's a favourite. The plant's markings create a dramatic pop – dark, tapering, thin leaves sprinkled with white stripes and bright dots.

 HOME GROWN

Native to southern Africa: Mozambique, Namibia, Lesotho, Swaziland and South Africa.

☀ **SUN**

Tolerates bright direct sun, bright indirect spots to partial shade, and can turn a darker colour or purple or red when in direct sun. It can scorch in hot climates in direct light.

 AIR

Likes dry to low humidity.

 WATER

Water roughly every 3–4 weeks and let the soil completely dry out between waterings. Spray the soil thoroughly at the base to wet but not saturate it. Late autumn to early spring is their dormant period so water less, roughly once every couple of months.

EASY-CARE HOUSEPLANTS

34

GROWING TOGETHER

The Zebra Haworthia's adorably chubby leaves are plump because they are storing water. Many cacti and succulents are composed of up to 90 per cent water and it's easy to forget about the water within — we are up to 60 per cent water, but our brains and hearts are 73 per cent water and our lungs 83 per cent. This internal H2O regulates our bodies and an adult needs to drink about eight glasses a day to keep healthily hydrated. Luckily this daily consumption can also come from foods such as porridge, soup, watermelon, cucumber, salad, yogurt and, yes, cacti and prickly pears (see recipes on page 106–118). Like plants, when we aren't properly hydrating, our skin and our insides wilt, putting unnecessary strain on our joints and organs. So, any time you are watering your plants, pour an extra one for yourself!

HAWORTHIA CONCOLOR

JADE PLANT

Crassula ovata

AKA:

*Lucky Plant,
Money Tree,
Chinese Money
Plant.*

The Jade Plant is a popular choice across Asia due to its association with bringing good luck, prosperity and wealth. According to feng shui, pop this money plant in a southeastern corner and it will bring good fortune. This little guy is super easy to propagate – new plant babies can be gifted to share the wealth.

Its thick stems and flat, plump leaves store water within the plant, hence its resilient reputation. It's also considered a survivor as these plants can tolerate most conditions and have very long life spans, usually being passed down for generations. I recently acquired a new addition, 'Wanda' – my friend remembers his mum bringing her home as a 5cm (2in) Jade in 1972 – she's now 1.22m (4ft) high. Kept in ideal conditions they can form pink or white star-shaped flowers in wintertime. Different variations of Jade Plants can show red, yellow or orange edges along the leaf tips.

 HOME GROWN

Native to KwaZulu-Natal and Eastern Cape provinces of South Africa and Mozambique.

 SUN

Prefers full sun to partial sun.

 AIR

Likes dry to low humidity.

 WATER

Water thoroughly every 3–4 weeks, but let the soil dry out between waterings. Water even more sparingly in autumn/winter, but if she looks wrinkly, it's a sign she's thirsty.

GROWING TOGETHER

Jade Plants lend themselves well to being used as bonsai beginners. Many think of bonsai as a specific type of tree, but the term 'bonsai' describes the Japanese art of pruning, training and cultivating plants to resemble miniature trees in shallow containers. The act of touching the plant as you slowly and delicately prune back the leaves or stems to create and sculpt the shape of a small tree is a very calming project and a great way to unwind. It's a perfect way to practise a little self-care as gardening reduces stress, anxiety, depression and loneliness. So, whether you have an outdoor space or not, this medieval Japanese technique is an urban gardening tip that's good for your mind, body and soul! You can easily propagate the cuttings from your Jade bonsai to make new plants too (see pages 80–85).

STRING OF PEARLS

Senecio rowleyanus

AKA:

*String of Beads,
String of Peas.*

These bubbly, beaded beauties are tactile plants. These spherical-shaped succulents are trailing wonders and I love seeing how people smile and react to their perfect pea-like resemblance. They are easy-peasy to propagate as they root effortlessly from cuttings. As they hold water in their bubble-like leaves they can withstand neglect, so hold back overwatering urges.

Each string has its own independent roots even though they are typically seen growing in a mass clump. In nature they tend to grow in bright and warm climates along rocky terrains, but as an indoor plant they are usually kept as a hanging plant or cascade vertically from a shelf, casting amazing shadows with their silhouette of thin vines and curvy orbs. In the summer they can blossom with unusual fluffy starburst white flowers that smell of cinnamon.

 HOME GROWN

Hails from southwest Africa.

 SUN

Thrives in direct sun, but can still survive bright, indirect to partial sun.

 AIR

Likes dry to low humidity.

 WATER

Water or spray soil thoroughly every 3–4 weeks, but let it dry out between waterings. Water sparingly in autumn/winter, but if the peas start to 'raisin', it's a sign to give her a little drink to moisten the soil.

GROWING TOGETHER

A beautiful lesson that flowering plants like String of Pearls teach us is how to let go. When they flower it's special and seasonal so they come and go. The flowers that graced you with their presence will, within a few weeks, start to wilt, yellow and eventually shrivel and perish. Once this happens you can leave the now extinguished flowers on the stem to eventually break down, dry, and drop off themselves.

Alternatively, you can pinch off the drying buds to remove the faded flowers to make room for the new — either for new blossoms to appear or for the plant to retain energy for new growth. You can place the perished flowers in the soil or at the base of the plant to help the old life bring new life with the nutrients. Nature shows us the cycle of rejuvenation and how newness arises from letting go of the old.

PRICKLY PEAR CACTUS
Opuntia varieties

FAVES:
Bunny Ear Cactus
AKA:
Polka Dot Cactus.

OPUNTIA ROBUSTA

Resist the urge to touch as although this cartoony cactus has soft and tactile-looking bunny ears, he's a prickly character indeed. This cactus is covered in glochids —soft-looking hairlike spikes that are thinner than human hair and barbed so when they stick to you they are tricky to remove and irritate the skin.

Plants in the Prickly Pear Cactus (aka Paddle Cactus) genus *Opuntia* do look like cacti designed by Dr Seuss, with their interesting shape, almost goofy silhouette and especially their diverse colours. They are beautiful beasts, but keep them out of reach of children and unwary guests who may not have had the pleasure of encountering these spiky shrubs.

 HOME GROWN

Native to central and northern Mexico.

 SUN

Loves a bright sunbathe and thrives in 4–6 hours of full sun daily, but can survive without direct sun in a filtered light setting.

 AIR

Likes dry to low humidity.

 WATER

Depending on the time of year and temperature, roughly once a month, but for warmer climates and hotter periods water every two weeks. Spray soil thoroughly but only when soil is bone dry. Ignore them late autumn to early spring during the dormant period, only watering lightly once or twice during winter.

MICRODASYS ALBISPINA

GROWING TOGETHER

There are many amazing health benefits to consuming and using Prickly Pear Cacti. Though not all types bear fruit, some aren't just delicious to eat, they are nutritious and healthy too as they are vitamin-rich and a natural antioxidant. Even the prickly pear seeds within the fruits themselves are incredibly useful. The increasingly popular prickly pear seed oil is effective for skin and hair care products due to its hydrating, healing, nourishing and anti-ageing properties. I love that every part of this crazy cool cactus can be used to hydrate and nourish our bodies inside and out.

TREE HOUSELEEKS

Aeonium varieties

FAVES:

Aeonium Sunburst,
Aeonium Kiwi,
Aeonium Garnet,
Silk Pinwheel.

Tree Houseleeks give the beautiful botanical succulent look that many desire, but these 'succas' are super adaptable. They can withstand many climates, from hot spots used for 'xeriscapes' (drought-tolerant landscape gardens) to moderate and wet ones. They are winter-hardy, but they prefer being frost-free so protect them during a freeze if outdoors. Aeoniums tend to be a popular pairing for rockeries around the world along with their closely related cousins Sempervivums, aka 'Hens and Chicks'.

'Aeonium' comes from the Ancient Greek word for 'ageless', and they are hardy succulents that, when kept indoors, enjoy a sunny windowsill. They grow with overlapping, usually plump, flat leaves to create a round rosette shape. Some varieties stay low growers while others grow upwards from long, thick stems with leggy branches and log-like tree bases as they mature.

 HOME GROWN

Many hail from the Canary Islands, but some are native to Morocco, Madeira, East Africa and Yemen and usually grow in rocky or mountain terrain.

SUN

Prefers bright full sun to partial shade.

 AIR

Likes low humidity.

 WATER

Water or spray soil thoroughly every 2–3 weeks when it is dry to the touch. Water sparingly during autumn and winter.

AEONIUM KIWI

SEMPERVIVUMS

TREE AEONIUM

GROWING TOGETHER

Nature and plants can offer daily reflections, and one way to enjoy a mindful pause is to consciously seek out a natural pattern called the Fibonacci spiral. The Fibonacci spiral, also known as the 'Golden Ratio', is basically nature's code describing the mathematical precision of plants growing symmetrically so that the leaves, petals or the plant get optimal sunlight. This natural geometry means that plants are designed to grow at the perfect ratio – the angles of the leaves overlap as little as possible to get as much light as possible. Examples of this natural order are all around us, creating beautiful shapes and patterns. These aren't just aesthetically pleasing; looking at them can relax and calm our brains too. You can soak up some satisfying Golden Ratio when you look down into the symmetry of the Aeoniums rosette shape and understand that Mother Nature created that perfect ratio so the plant would grow flawlessly.

WE ARE FORGED FROM NATURE.

STRING OF HEARTS
Ceropegia woodii

AKA:

*Chain of Hearts,
Rosary Vine,
Sweetheart Vine.*

This beauty is fast-growing and nicknamed for its heart-shaped leaves. The String of Hearts is a trailing succulent that clings and crawls along soil and rocks in its natural wooded terrain. Its roots develop at the nodes of the shoots which help it to spread and latch on to surfaces to grow along. Plants such as String of Hearts with stems that create new roots and shoots from their nodes are called rhizomes – derived from Ancient Greek meaning 'to cause to strike root'.

String of Hearts makes a stunning hanging plant and these rhizomes allow it to keep growing downwards, cascading into a lush green waterfall. The little sweetheart leaves have a dappled pattern of deep green laced with metallic silver, but other varieties can be seen in purple, pink, white and green combinations. In the summer they can produce strange bulbous elongated pale purple florals.

HOME GROWN

Found among woodlands in South Africa, Swaziland and Zimbabwe.

 SUN

Desires a bright spot, but filtered natural light, not direct sun.

 AIR

Likes low humidity.

 WATER

Water every 7–10 days, but let the soil dry out between waterings. It stores water in tubers (swollen underground stems) so can deal with underwatering versus overwatering.

GROWING TOGETHER

A little creative and playful activity you can do is to sketch the pattern in the middle of the sweetheart leaf. You don't have to be an artist trying to paint a still life, this exercise is about letting go and drawing the patterns and shapes occurring within nature – let your mind wander and discover what else you see within the lines and pattern. Treat this like trying to see shapes in clouds and let your inner creative child run free without fear or worry of the outcome of your sketch. I sometimes think these leaves remind me of shells or landscapes from an aeroplane. What do you see?

PRAYER PLANT

Maranta leuconeura

AKA:

*Maranta,
Herringbone Plant.*

Ah, the stunner that is the Prayer Plant; look at her with her exotic colours like a neon dream. The Prayer Plant is queen of the rainforest at Hi Cacti as she's our most popular houseplant. From the lime green centre of her oval leaves she flares out hot pink pin-striped veins that look like they are hand-painted against the velvety dark green leaf.

Not only are the colours of this eye-catching plant pretty mesmerizing, but so are her moves – yes, she literally moves. Her Prayer Plant name comes from her opening up and spreading her leaves out flat during the day to catch sunlight and then closing them upwards and together like hands in prayer at night. This is an example of a 'diurnal rhythm', in which some plants follow a repeating 24-hour cycle in sync with the Earth's rotation, like their own internal clock. So, these dramatically painted-leafed plants literally dance to the Earth's rotational rhythm to soak up the sunlight.

HOME GROWN

Hails from the tropical rainforests of Brazil.

 ### SUN

Enjoys medium to bright filtered sunlight, not direct sun.

 ### AIR

Likes moderate humidity and an occasional misting.

 ### WATER

Water about once a week, but let the soil dry slightly – 5cm (2in) deep – before watering.

GROWING TOGETHER

The way that Prayer Plants open themselves up to catch the sun and start their day to soak up life and light is a beautiful reminder to reflect on how we set ourselves up for our day. The way we treat ourselves both physically and mentally first thing in the morning can really help us to start on the 'right side of the bed'. One direct inspiration we can take from this plant is to start our day slowly, rising to face the sun with

a short meditation (even just five minutes) with your hands together in front of your heart. Science-backed research shows that even a short daily meditation can increase your attention span, boost your mood, improve sleep, decrease blood pressure, increase pain tolerance, decrease stress and anxiety — and much more. Even if you aren't there yet with meditation, just beginning your day sitting quietly for five minutes or with a cup of tea facing the sun is meditative.

BRAZILIAN BUTTERFLIES

Oxalis triangularis

AKA:

Love Plant,
Purple Shamrock,
False Shamrock.

Beautiful, bold and bulb-acious, Brazilian Butterflies are known for their unique shamrock shape and purple and burgundy leaves. The leaves open up during the daytime to catch the sun and close up like cocktail umbrellas at night or in a draught to protect themselves. This means they are photophilic – the botanical term for when a plant opens and closes its leaves in response to light. When closed, their delicate leaves resemble butterflies. Underground, their roots are bulbs that resemble little pine cones.

In spring, during their growing period, they form new leaves and will also bloom with small bell-shaped flowers in either yellow or pale lilac depending on the variety. The leaves and flowers are edible with a slight citrus flavour to add a little decadent houseplant touch to your next baking project or a salad.

HOME GROWN

Native to several countries in southern South America including Brazil.

SUN

Desires a bright spot, but indirect or filtered natural light. Direct sun can burn the leaves.

AIR

Likes normal/moderate humidity.

WATER

Water weekly but 'touch test' the top 5cm (2in) to allow it to dry between waterings as these bulb-based plants can be vulnerable to overwatering. Water sparsely during the dormant winter period – about once a month.

GROWING TOGETHER

A little life lesson these Butterflies remind us of is patience. Even the Oxalis sometimes needs a break, so hold tight, be patient and don't take it personally. Brazilian Butterflies occasionally go dormant, looking like the entire plant has died — no stems, no butterflies. But don't fret or toss your baby in the bin — just move the plant to a slightly more shaded spot, stop watering and let the soil thoroughly dry. Have faith in knowing the bulbs are still hiding under the soil and they will re-emerge. In a few weeks, you will see a new leaf peeping through. That is the time to resume watering and move it back to a bright spot with filtered light. Soon, your purple butterflies will return lush and revived, literally rising from the ashes — well, soil actually. For any disappointment you feel if and when this does happen, usually only once every few years, you will appreciate watching it return to its glory.

SPOTTED BEGONIA

Begonia maculata

AKA:

Polka Dot Begonia, Angel Wing Begonia, Clown Begonia.

In my humble opinion, the Spotted Begonia is one of the most striking houseplants. The large wing-shaped leaves have a crimson red underbelly like a Louboutin stiletto, which provides a dramatic contrast to the olive-green fronts speckled with white spots that look like they've been hand-painted. From spring and autumn it produces clusters of white to pale pink flowers shaped like pilgrims' bonnets.

Spotted Begonias grow satisfyingly quickly and vertically upwards to heights of more than 1m (39in) – this can be avoided by pruning twice a year. They come from a big plant family with over 1,500 different species and produce one of the smallest seeds in the world – so small that they look like dust.

HOME GROWN

Hails from the tropical forests of Brazil, but was only first discovered in 1982. Originally native to Mexico, Asia, South Africa and Central America.

 ### SUN

Desires filtered sun to light shade; direct sun can bleach or burn the leaves.

 ### AIR

Likes normal to moderate humidity, but do not mist. Avoid draughts or heaters in winter.

 ### WATER

Thoroughly water weekly. 'Touch test' to check the top 5cm (2in) of soil is dry before watering. Water less in winter – twice a month. Increase watering if the leaf tips are browning or dry.

GROWING TOGETHER

Spotted Begonias, like many plants, grow towards the sun to soak up the light. Facing the sun to grow is a beautiful analogy for people as well. Whether you wake up to a sunny day or not, there is a way you can help yourself to start on the sunny side of life daily, which is with gratitude. Beginning your day by thinking of three things that you are grateful for helps to light a fire within you and starts your day on a positive foot.

Practising gratitude is shown to pave new neurological pathways that help you create more happy hormones. Gratitudes are also linked to a restful night's sleep, lowering stress and the promotion of positivity. To give this exercise more power, write the gratitudes down as this strengthens the process. You could even start a gratitude notebook; if you struggle sometimes with depression, addiction or anxiety, this can be a reflective and helpful tool to see the positives on days when you can't quite find the sun.

CHEESE PLANT

Monstera deliciosa

AKA:

Swiss Cheese Plant.

The Cheese Plant is a houseplant staple – simple to look after, shows you signs of what it wants, grows quickly and propagates easily. Its scientific name doesn't lie, these *Monsteras* can grow monstrously big – up to 9m (30ft) high – but don't worry, the maximum height is usually 3m (10ft) when kept indoors.

Cheese Plants are a great way to add big greenery and leafy foliage that will keep going and grow with ease into a space. Young Cheese Plants start with medium-sized heart-shaped leaves, but as they grow their leaves start to split and get their 'Swiss cheese' holes. These guys are climbers so for indoor use you may need a moss pole to hold them upright.

 HOME GROWN

Originally hung out in tropical forests of southern Mexico, Belize, Honduras, Costa Rica, Guatemala and south down to Panama.

☀ **SUN**

Prefers a bright spot, but with filtered, dappled sunlight; strong direct sun can bleach out or burn the leaves.

 AIR

Prefers moderate humidity, but can tolerate normal air with occasional misting.

 WATER

Check the top 5cm (2in) of soil is dry before watering and water weekly. The leaves wilt slightly when thirsty; brown or dry leaf tips are a sign of lack of water or misting. Water less during the winter period, twice a month.

MONKEY MASK MONSTERA

AERIAL ROOTS FOR CLIMBING

These are different to the actual roots and aren't a sign that your plant needs to be repotted. Extra or large aerial roots that appear on your indoor plant can be a sign that it needs more light as they will grow to try and pull the plant towards more of a light source. You can remove excess or large aerials without harming the plant – if they aren't needed for climbing they will take up the plant's energy – but a few aerials here and there are natural. In nature they scale large trees using their aerial roots to latch on to surfaces to grow and spread, almost like ivy, but much bigger. Their aerial roots can be so long and strong that they have traditionally been used to make rope or baskets in Mexico and Peru.

GROWING TOGETHER

The Cheese Plant's trademark splits and holes are not just fun but also functional, allowing sunlight to pass through dense leaves to get to the base of the plant, so the entire plant gets sufficient energy. These holes also allow rainfall to pass through and trickle down to the roots of the plant. The bigger the leaves grow, the hole-ier they are so they don't block the plant's sun and water supplies. This clever natural design is a great reminder of balance and how we should ensure that all parts of ourselves and our life are getting enough attention, energy and light. Try and make room to share out time, effort and energy to create your own grounded and healthy version of yourself. If we allow one part of our life to become too big – like these Monstera leaves – it might block out light, nutrients or energy from the other parts that help us to be healthy and well rounded.

PANCAKE PLANT

Pilea peperomioides

AKA:

*Pass It On Plant,
UFO Plant,
Friendship Plant,
Coin Plant,
Missionary Plant,
Chinese Money
Plant.*

RAINDROP PILEA

With its bubbly and shiny leaves and perky, cheerful stance you just can't help but smile when you see this odd-looking plant. Pancake Plants keep giving based on their ease to grow, simple propagation and new plant babies that pop up. They are popular among plant enthusiasts, designers and photographers with their weird and wonderful shape and silhouette.

These guys are super easy, grow quickly and, luckily, tell you when they need watering as the leaves droop slightly when they are thirsty and 'ping' right back up the next day after a drink. Despite its *'peperomioides'* name it's not a type of *Peperomia* — it was named as such by botanists because it resembled the *Peperomia* genus so much, but is oddly enough in the nettle family.

 HOME GROWN

Found in foothills of the Himalayan Mountains, native to Sichuan and Yunnan provinces in southern China.

SUN

Desires moderate light, bright but indirect dappled or filtered light. Direct sun can burn the leaves.

 AIR

Likes humidity so enjoys an occasional mist if not in a humid spot.

 WATER

Water weekly and thoroughly but allow the top 5cm (2in) of soil to dry slightly between waterings.

PILEA PEPEROMIOIDES

GROWING TOGETHER

The other nicknames Pass It On Plant or Friendship Plant refer to how easy it is to spread the love. Sharing is caring and this plant is a great and green way to connect people, being simple to propagate and the ease and speed with which it 'pops up' new plant babies. Gifting a baby from your mama plant is a friendly way to give a pick-me-up to someone who might appreciate it or need it. Whether it's to say 'hello' to an elderly neighbour, welcome a new colleague, a token thank-you or just 'thinking of you' gift. Kindness spreads kindness, and think how this little ray of sunshine of a plant could brighten someone's day and the pleasure they could get from watching it grow — literally a breath of fresh air you can share with someone.

GROWING WELL–ROUNDED

Pileas grow and lean towards sunlight, so to create an evenly shaped plant, give her a little spin or turn occasionally. Many plants bend or turn towards the sun to aid their survival, but some more than others. The fancy botany term (aka plant lingo) for this is phototropism (photo: light, tropism: turning).

SNAKE PLANT

Sansevieria varieties

FAVES:

Spaghetti Sansevieria, Mikado African Spear, Starfish, Moonshine, Black Coral, Whale Fin.

SANSEVIERIA TRIFASCIATA LAURENTII

This is the plant with a bold silhouette and die-hard tendencies – it's a tough cookie. The Snake Plant's leaves grow vertically upright and have a strong silhouette of organic curves that remind me of green patterned flames lined with bold, bright yellow markings. These statuesque *Sansevierias* have amazing varieties of shapes and colours, and you will see them across a multitude of settings because they're extremely low maintenance, very flexible on lighting, and forgiving of erratic waterings.

Their tough and strong leaves grow tall and thin so are great for small spaces as they grow well when leaves are potted closely together. This bladed beauty is technically succulent and with its lighting flexibility can survive in many settings, but will grow faster in strong natural light and slower in low light.

 HOME GROWN

Native to Africa, Madagascar and south Asia.

 SUN

Prefers medium light, bright but indirect filtered light. It can tolerate low light and strong light, but avoid too much direct sun.

 AIR

Very versatile, okay with dry air and can tolerate humidity.

 WATER

Allow soil to completely dry between waterings and needs good drainage. Water every two weeks, but can tolerate droughts of up to eight weeks so great for out-of-towners or slackers.

STARFISH SANSEVIERIA

SANSEVIERIA ZEYLANICA

GROWING TOGETHER

Sansevierias have adapted an unusual form of photosynthesis (Crassulacean Acid Metabolism for the science curios out there) in order to retain water during the day. This process means they release oxygen and absorb carbon dioxide during the night, while most plants release oxygen during the daytime and at night take in oxygen and release carbon dioxide. So, Snake Plants give a boost of oxygen while you sleep that can leave you feeling refreshed at night, while simultaneously absorbing toxins from the air to aid a restful sleep. This helpful bedroom buddy is one of the most powerful air purifiers, and NASA's research shows that it removes most air pollutants including formaldehyde, xylene, toluene, benzene and trichloroethylene. Powerhouse plant indeed.

PRACTICAL PAL

In Africa, Snake Plant leaves can be used to create hemp or to their fibres to make rope and some *Sansevieria* species has antiseptic properties so was traditionally used to make bandages.

ZZ PLANT

Zamioculcas zamiifolia

AKA:

Zanzibar Gem,
Zuzu Plant,
Emerald Palm.

This majestic plant has thick gem-shaped leaves that are so glossy it often gets mistaken for a fake plant. ZZ Plants grow compact, long, upright stems lined with waxy green leaves; youthful leaves are lime green and turn a dark emerald colour with maturity. New stems begin with the leaves tightly wound against the branch and look like a spike before they fan out.

ZZ Plants can grow to up to 75cm (30in) tall, but their upright and compact-growing nature means you can share your space without them taking over. They have bulbous rhizomes hidden just slightly under the soil surface. These bulbs act like water tanks, allowing the plant to survive up to four months without water, so water sparsely – perfect for those who go away for long periods or neglect watering needs.

HOME GROWN

Originally found in Zanzibar and eastern Africa from south Kenya to northeast South Africa.

SUN

Prefers moderate filtered light to partial shade, but is versatile to most light conditions. Low light-tolerant but avoid direct intense sun.

AIR

Likes low humidity, so can tolerate dry air and most conditions.

WATER

Water approximately every three weeks, allowing the top 5cm (2in) of soil to dry out completely between waterings. Water less during the winter, about once a month.

GROWING TOGETHER

This is another inspiring air-purifying plant that releases a lot of fresh and boosting oxygen due to the canopy created by the fanning of their leaves. They are also powerful at removing volatile indoor air pollutants. Next time you need to let go of some tension, go take a little breather with your purifying plant. Create your own green Zen den, whether at work or home, to enjoy the company of some purifying houseplants and seek a moment of relaxing refuge. Simply sit and focus on your breathing. Breathe in deeply through the nose, hold at the top for five seconds, then exhale slowly through pursed lips either quietly or making a sigh of relief. When we take a minute to focus on breathing deeply and slowly this can be very calming for your brain, body and nervous system.

PET–FRIENDLY PLANTS

PLANT PALS FOR YOUR FURRY FRIENDS

Some pets aren't interested in houseplants, but only you know your pet best. I have my little wire-haired dachshund Otto (a pampered pooch that is literally our baby) and he is constantly around all types of plant pals, toxic or not, and pays them no mind. Most of the time, even if your pet did eat a toxic houseplant it would only be enough to make them feel some discomfort or mouth irritation such as drooling. Houseplants described as 'toxic to pets' are only really mildly toxic and a pet would have to eat a large amount to do any damage. It's more likely that your pets would get severely sick if they got into a bouquet of flowers such as daffodils, lilies or mistletoe rather than toxic houseplants. You can keep plants out of their reach or in closed-off rooms, but here are some of our favourite pet-safe plants and a few tips to keep your fur babies safe.

PLANTS FOR FURRY FRIENDS THAT CHEW

Pancake Plant (see page 56), Bird's Nest Fern, Haworthias (see page 34), Peperomias, Boston Fern, Christmas Cactus, Echeverias, Parlour Palms, Spider Plant, Ponytail Palm, Aspidistra, Prayer Plant (see page 48), Musa Banana Plant, Calatheas, Fittonias, Polka Dot Plant, Areca Palm and Bromeliads.

TIPS

- A deterrent for curious cats is to put mothballs in a small container with holes near or behind the plant.

- Some pets are attracted to the soil in the pot rather than the plant, so try topping the soil with gravel or stones.

- Sprinkle coffee grains, chillies or citrus peel over the soil to deter pets.

- Sharp or bitter flavours or scents are off-putting to pets so you can either buy deterrent pet sprays or make your own by using 1 part citronella oil to 10 parts water. Or 1 part white vinegar to 2 parts apple cider vinegar.

- Put toothpicks or wooden skewers with pointed edges around the inside edge of the pot to create a hindrance for pets.

MINDFUL EXERCISE

TAKE A MOMENT TO GIVE THANKS TO NATURE

Try and notice five things you use throughout your day that are aided by the power of plants. Think of it as an exercise where you mindfully turn over to the ingredients panel of the back of your day. Picture the big and small ways in which plants are present in your actions and fuel your day without you even thinking about them. Even something as simple as putting on your cotton socks and taking a moment to envision a cotton field growing to help produce them – feel the gratitude for the ways that the cotton plant provides for you. And that 'pick-me-up' coffee in your cup is thanks to the nutrient-rich volcanic soils of Colombia bearing fruitful gifts.

A LESSON FROM NATURE

Gratefully. we can depend on nature to share with us many life lessons when we stop to slow down and tune in. Her petals, oils, seeds, roots, fruits, barks and air have been fuelling our ancestors and our journey since the beginning, and we can continue to utilize plant life in our daily lives. With a new-found appreciation we can embrace the idea that bringing plant life from the outside to the indoors can nourish our happiness, minds and mental health as much as our bodies.

CHAPTER 2

PLANT HACKS & KNACKS

Taking care of your plants is a way to take care of yourself by slowing down and connecting to the vibrations of nature from the comfort of your home. As you go through the flow of plant care, try to do so in a thoughtful and mindful manner, enjoying the process of growing and nurturing them. Here are some hacks and tips to keep your plants happy and healthy so they will gratefully reflect wellbeing and positivity right back at you.

SPIRALLED CEREUS CACTUS

PLANT CARE & SELF-CARE RITUALS
BLOOM & THRIVE WITH YOUR PLANTS

Coming up with a little ritual around your plant care can help both you and your plants thrive. Start by having a set day each week where you 'check in' with your plants – water any that seem thirsty, remove old leaves or buds, check for potential pests and maybe give leaves that need it a little mist or clean. While you do that you can 'check in' with yourself and reflect on your own needs.

Before you start your plant-care session you could make yourself a tea or coffee and maybe do a short meditation to settle yourself into the moment – see Root to Rise on page 68 or the Tea Meditation on page 112 for some inspiration. This routine will help make your plant-care experience go from chore to pleasurable, relaxing self-care downtime. From a practical point of view, designating a little time on a set day each week helps you to regulate watering habits and to nip any plant-care issues, such as pests, in the bud.

SING TO YOUR PLANTS

Heard that talking to your plants is good for them? Well, another outlet is to sing, so put on your favourite tunes and sing along while you care for your plants. There's evidence that plants respond positively to music, and singing is good for your wellbeing too – it increases oxygen intake, boosts happiness and decreases stress hormones. I personally sound like a train wreck when I sing, but it feels great and is a release, so it's good to know it also helps your plants grow – luckily, they won't judge your pitch while you let your hair down.

SETTING UP YOUR PLANT-CARE ROUTINE

Find a day or time that suits your needs. My plant-care day is Sunday, as that's my day off and creating a ritual around my plant care helps me make room to pause. Some simple self-care rituals I've added to my plant care are putting something nostalgic on my record player (usually The Beatles as my dad and I used to sing along to them together), lighting incense and candles, and having a cup of my favourite tea while my plants have a little soak in the bathtub (see page 70). Afterwards I usually have a bath myself and add some botanicals such as petals and soak salts. You might find setting aside a particular day each week hard, so try incorporating your regular plant- and self-care ritual into an evening to help you relax after a full-on day.

Other plant-care rituals might be monthly, such as giving your plants a feed or tending to plants with monthly watering needs, such as cacti and succulents. It helps to choose a specific and memorable day each month to do this, such as the first or last day of the month, pay day or a birthday number. Setting an intentional space and time to nurture yourself and your plants will cultivate you both.

SPREAD THE LOVE

Your ritual doesn't have to be a solo project. You might want to experience the green scene with others in your life, whether it's sharing the knowledge with a child or quality time with a housemate. Plant-care benefits are for everyone, young and old, and by partaking in this cathartic time and ritual together you are sharing the wellbeing effects with those you love as well.

ROOT TO RISE MEDITATION

BREATHE AND CONNECT TO NATURE

This meditation was written by Lol Swift, a Mindfulness Practitioner and Transformational Life Coach who also hosts women's circles and retreat events. Lol and I have shared numerous conversations about nature as a soother and the many stimulating effects and benefits being in nature has on wellbeing and health. These effects translate to keeping houseplants, which create a daily connection to the natural world. One of Lol's passions and specialities is offering practices of mindfulness and meditation to beginners in ways that make the practices simple, relatable and accessible. Whether you are a seasoned meditator or a new kid on the block, enjoy this step-by-step break to breathe, go inward and connect to nature alongside your plants.

- Position yourself in front of one or more of your plants. Find a comfortable seat, either cross-legged or sitting on a chair with your palms resting softly on your knees.
- Breathe in slowly through your nose as you draw your shoulders up to your ears. As you exhale with a sigh through the mouth, drop your shoulders away from the ears and repeat this step three times.
- Slow the breath right down and trace it as it enters through the nose and travels down the body, landing gently in the belly, acting as an anchor to ground you in the moment. Empty the belly and follow the breath on its journey back up the body and out through the nose. Allow yourself to soften and let go with the exhalation. Stay here for a minute or two and whenever the mind wanders, simply bring the focus back to the breath and to the rise and fall of the belly.
- With a soft and gentle gaze, observe your plants in front of you. Notice the colours, the shades, the shapes, the patterns, the textures. Take it all in, scan every part of the plants with curiosity. Stay here a while, simply observing and connecting to your plants. How does it feel to be witnessing them? What feelings does it evoke?

- As you gently close your eyes and slow down the breath, start to feel your connection to the surface below you and how it supports you. This is your point of connection with the earth. With each exhalation allow yourself to be fully held and supported by Mother Earth. Sink into it. Let go.
- Imagine yourself as a plant, roots growing from your tailbone or your feet, travelling down, deep down into the soil, into the earth. As your roots reach deep, they connect you to the earth and bring you stability and strength. You feel anchored and are rooted deeply in your connection with Mother Nature.
- As you breathe in deeply, imagine your roots drawing all of the energy and nutrients that you need from the earth up through your body. With this rooting down, you are able to rise up with strength. The energy and nourishment drawn from your stable roots and the earth allows you to bloom and blossom, upwards and outwards from your crown. Imagine leaves unfurling. Full, luscious leaves and flowers bursting into bloom. Here you are, blooming. Tall. Proud. You in all your glory, all your fullness, here right now, thriving and rising into your fullest potential and expression.

Imagine the warm, golden sun shining down on you from above as you reach towards it. Reaching up high into the sky above, as high as you can imagine, as high as you dare to dream. And as you grow tall, root down deep so that you may anchor and then rise some more. Rise, rise, rise. Stay here for as long as you wish, enjoying this connection and union between the earth and the sky.
- Whenever you feel ready, take your hands and rub them together to generate some heat then cup them over your eyes. Enjoy the stillness and peace that the darkness brings.
- Take a few deep breaths here then gently remove your hands. With your eyes still closed, take some slow and gentle movements to softly wake the body back up and then flicker open your eyes.
- Place your hands over your heart and gaze softly at your plants. Thank them for their gifts, their wisdom and the lessons that they teach you.
- Remember that you can come back to this place of calm any time you like simply by placing your hand on your heart, taking a moment to connect with nature and imagining yourself rooting down to rise.

WATERING HACKS
WATERING MADE EASY

Whether they are thirsty types or drought survivors, when we bring plants indoors they depend on us to bring the rain to them. Here are a few tips to take some guesswork out of the 'to water or not to water' debate.

BATH TIME

A great way to allow all your thirsty plants to have a drink easily and quickly is to let them help themselves. Letting your houseplants 'bottom feed' the amount of water they need takes the guesswork out of how much water your plants want.

Put all your regular houseplants in the bathtub and run enough water to reach the bottom of the plants' roots. This can vary depending on the size of the pots and plants, but use your judgment – roughly 5–7cm (2–3in) from the bottom of the plant pot will usually suffice. Then leave your plants to sit in the water for 10–20 minutes to suck up as much as they fancy. If you don't have a bathtub (or to save water if you have fewer plants), you can do this in a sink.

Avoid this with cacti and succulents as they have minimal watering needs and can be more prone to root rot.

RAINDROPS KEEP FALLING ON MY PLANTS

Tap water is fine but the BEST way to water plants is distilled or rain water for a more natural drink. Giving your houseplants a natural shower is another great way to benefit your plants while being easy on your wallet and the environment. If you have the space, pop your houseplants outside during the next rainfall for up to half an hour. This will give them some pure water and cleans their leaves of dust particles too. However, don't do this during high winds or cold temperatures as this will damage the plants. When you bring them inside give the leaves a wipe down to avoid any blotchy marks, and this will be an enjoyable, mindful and calming activity for you as well.

To avoid moving plants in and out, put a bucket or trough out to collect fresh rainwater, but avoid using water that has sat for too long. Your plants will enjoy this natural rainwater as it doesn't contain chemicals typically found in tap water such as salt, chlorine or fluoride, which can be harsh to some plants. Reducing your tap water use doesn't just lessen your water bill, it reduces the strain on community utilities and helps protect the groundwater table and levels of your nearby rivers and lakes. Also, harvesting rainfall can reduce rainwater runoff, which can lead to local floods and soil erosion.

SAVE WATER, SHOWER TOGETHER

Share the steamy love and shower with your humidity-loving houseplants. Plants that hail from tropical rainforest climates thrive in a bit of humidity, which you can replicate with an occasional misting or humidifier, but combining your greens and your bathing habits can kill two birds with one stone, and also save water and energy. Sit some plants on the edges of your shower or bathtub or on any ledges or shelves in the bathroom to soak up a little steam while you are showering or bathing. Plants such as ferns, Prayer Plants and Cheese Plants will be grateful for some time in the humid air that will remind them of home, and you will create a lovely green microclimate of calm during your downtime as well. This can be a good hack for plants that like an occasional misting and will to help clean dust off your leafy pals too.

WATERING WHILE YOU'RE AWAY

PLANT CARE FROM AFAR

Here are a few tricks to help water your roommates while you are away. Firstly, give all your plants a thorough drink. Also consider moving plants that can tolerate it a bit further from sunlight so they do not dry out as quickly.

HOLIDAY WATERING TIPS

- **SHARING IS CARING** – if possible, move all your plants to the same spot so they can create a little microclimate.
- **BOTTLE METHOD** – a good way to upcycle large plastic or wine bottles. Make a small hole in the bottle top or cork by tapping a small nail or screw through the centre with a hammer – enough so water can drip out slowly (or use a corkscrew to go all the way through a cork). Put the cork or cap back on a full bottle of water and quickly invert it into the soil of your plant – deep enough to keep the bottle upright. The small hole and narrow funnelled neck allows the soil to pull water from the opening as it dries.
- **STRING METHOD** – fill up a container, bottle or vase with water and submerge one end of a 6mm (¼ in) braided nylon cord (or other absorbent cord) so that it touches the bottom of the container. Pot the other end of the string into the soil of your plant at least 7cm (3in) deep. This cord will carry moisture into the plant through the wick.
- **NEWSPAPER METHOD** – for large potted plants add several layers of damp newspaper to cover the top of the soil.
- **PLASTIC POT METHOD** – for clay, ceramic or other porous pots, temporarily repot plants into plastic pots to help them retain moisture.
- **ROCK METHOD** – for potted plants with drainage holes. Add small pebbles or stones to a shallow tray. Fill the tray with enough water to cover the top of the stones slightly and place potted plants on top.
- **SINK TRICK** – fill the kitchen sink with water and place a towel on the draining board with one end sitting in the water. Place your pots on the towel-covered counter and it will pull moisture to the plants. This is only suitable if the sink area provides adequate lighting for your plants.

HOW TO AVOID OVERWATERING

HOW NOT TO KILL YOUR HOUSEPLANT

Overloving or killing your plant with kindness can lead to some plant perils. Overwatering during the dormant winter months can be deadly, so lighten up and water less often during the wintertime. Another common plant crime is trying to Overloving or killing your plant with kindness can lead to some plant perils.

Overwatering during the dormantwinter months can be deadly, so lightenup and water less often during thewintertime. Another common plantcrime is trying to compensate for any neglect by drowning your plant. Easy does it, but if you find yourself with an overwatering woe, here are some tips to remedy the situation.

- **REPOT** – massage out the wet or damp soil from in and around the roots and repot your plant into fresh, dry soil and hold off watering for about a week or so.

- **MOVE** – relocate your plant to a warmer, brighter spot to help it dry out quicker.

- **DRY NEWSPAPER METHOD** – remove the plant from the container and wrap a layer of newspaper around the soil or root ball (or another dry material that can help absorb the excess moisture).

- **AERATE** – carefully poke a few holes in and around the plant's soil with a pencil or stick. This allows more air into the soil to speed up the drying process, but be gentle to avoid damaging roots.

TIPS FOR FORGETFUL WATERING TYPES

- **MOISTURE READERS** – these readers can help beginners and experts alike to figure out: 'To water or not to water, that is the question'. Some meters also gauge moisture levels based on plant types, which can add some more precision to your watering habits.

- **SELF-WATERING PLANTERS** – yes, these magical inventions do exist but can cost a pretty penny. If you are a house-plant lover and a busy bee or an out-of-towner, this could be an ideal 'cheat' for you.

- **PLAY TO YOUR STRENGTHS** – it might seem obvious, but a tip I often recommend to customers is to choose plants that suit your needs. If you tend to overwater then select more moisture-loving plants like Peace Lilies, Cheese Plants or other tropical, humidity-loving plants. If you underwater, go for plants that hail from the lands of drought such as cacti, *Sansevierias*, ZZ Plants and succulents.

PESTS & DISEASES

SIGNS THAT YOUR PLANT IS UNHAPPY

Disease or pests can occur at many stages of a plant's journey, before it even gets to a plant shop or to your home. If a plant has been neglected it can make them more susceptible to pests or disease as well. Some of the following care culprits can make your plant more prone to disease and pests:

- **OVERWATERING** – pests can be attracted to decaying roots in soggy soil.
- **LACK OF LIGHT** – if it is depleted of enough sunlight this can weaken the plant. Even a build-up of dust particles on leaves can block sunlight, so give them an occasional dust with a damp cloth.
- **ROOT–BOUND PLANTS** – roots that have outgrown their space can deplete nutrients and make the plant more vulnerable to disease. Repotting your plant gives the roots more room and replenishes it with fresh nutrient-rich soil, which makes a happy plant.

CHECKING FOR NASTIES

Signs of a plant's good health can show on its leaves. If you see yellowing or brown patches or marks on the leaves, this could mean a virus or disease is lurking. Also, investigate under leaves as these and the soil can show hints of diseases or pests – moulds, flies, scales, white dots or powdery, fluffy white residues can be marks of your plant pal being unwell. Prevention is great, but all is not lost if you spot signs early on, which is another good reason to look over, touch and check in with your plants regularly – do not leave a leaf unturned (sorry, I couldn't skip that plant pun, it was too good!).

A FEW TIPS TO CURE

- First isolate the plant to prevent it from spreading disease to your other plants.
- If a pest or disease is only lurking on one part of the plant, remove or prune off that part to prevent it from spreading.
- For gnats or flies, get rid of the infected soil quickly and repot with new soil or spray soapy water (add a few drops of washing-up liquid to water) on top of the infected soil. Use top dressing such as shells or gravel to cover the soil.
- For pests such as aphids, mealybugs, scale insects or spider mites, use soapy water in a spray bottle to shoot off and dislodge pests in and around affected areas. Use a toothpick to remove any further nasties hiding in tight spots. You might have to repeat this treatment again if you see any returning signs.
- To remove mealybugs, use a cotton bud dipped in methylated spirits. Wipe wherever you find the bugs and their fluffy white residue in and about the base of the plant and stem cracks.

MAMMILLARIA CACTUS

PLANT CARE IS SELF CARE.

SOIL & FEED

KEEPING YOUR PLANT WELL FED

SOIL

Most houseplants are fine with standard multipurpose soil or compost. New soil contains a mixture that can keep your plant feeling fresh and nutrient-rich for about six months. Multipurpose soil usually contains moisture-holding organic matter and some fertilizing additives, which makes it great for most houseplants, but not ideal for cacti and succulents. You can get cacti- and succulent-specific soil which has better drainage and the right pH balance of acidity and alkalinity for happy cacti. You can use regular potting soil for cacti and succulents, but you will need to add drainage additives as this type of soil will retain too much moisture.

FEED

Feed can typically be purchased as a liquid fertilizer or as a powder that you add to water to dilute. But give your plant a drink of water first to moisten the soil – dry soil won't allow roots to absorb the nutrients in the feed.

Don't go crazy. Overfeeding your houseplants can have negative effects such as browning leaves and tips, and it can weaken the plant, making it susceptible to disease or pests. Feed plants regularly from March to September, about once or twice a month, but plants only really need to feed in the summertime, which is the height of their growing period.

If you have repotted a plant recently with fresh soil, this can contain enough nutrients for about 3–6 months. There are also speciality feeds for certain types of plants, so if that is your bag, go for it, but just a regular plant feed is fine to use. Learn to make your own DIY natural plant feed on page 90.

DRAINAGE

Good drainage is key. Pot into a planter with a drainage hole or create drainage layers by adding aerating mixes such as gravel, pebbles, perlite, vermiculite, bark or other organic materials. This creates room for roots to grow, letting air, nutrients and moisture to flow so the plant can breathe easy. See advice on pots and drainage on page 131.

REPOTTING

REHOMING FOR A HEALTHY PLANT

Giving your plants more room and the fresh nutrients of new soil will help them grow faster, healthier and to their fullest potential. Typically when repotting your plant if you want to encourage growth go 1-2 inches up in pot size diameter at a time.

There are benefits for you too – this practice is calming and there is something very grounding about getting your hands dirty when you are repotting. Delicately handling the roots creates a connection to the natural world within the comfort of your own home. Studies show that if a person repots a plant, they are more likely to keep it alive, as the act of handling and caring for a plant makes them feel more committed to its health. When you next repot, take time to mindfully enjoy the process, knowing that this deed is going to help your plant flourish and bloom. Reflect on how you too can make space in your 'pot' and what enriching nutrients you can add to your 'mix' to enable yourself to bloom.

WHEN TO REPOT

The best time to repot houseplants is early in their growing period, which for most is spring. Many plants won't like being repotted during dormant periods. Autumn to winter is when your plants are hibernating so they don't need as much water, they don't want

feed and they don't really want you to move them around or fuss with them much – they are having a little rest until they begin their growing period again come springtime and summer.

WHAT ARE SIGNS IT'S TIME TO REPOT?

If you see the roots at the top or bottom of the soil then it needs to go up a pot size. Check if the roots have reached the side walls of the pot by carefully popping your plant out of the pot. When roots start to reach any of the pot walls, your houseplant will be happy to receive about 5cm (2in) of new soil around the roots to grow.

Repotting isn't just needed if the roots have outgrown the pot. For your plant to thrive, it's still ideal to repot every year or so to give it nutrients from a fresh batch of soil. You can then just remove the top couple of inches of soil and add new soil on top to replenish.

GIVE IT A SQUEEZE

If removing your plants from the pot is tricky, a tip for those in plastic pots is to give the pot a little squeeze all around it to loosen the plant, or gently tap the side of the pot to remove it more easily.

PROPAGATION NATION

SPREAD THE PLANT LOVE

Propagating is a way to grow your collection by cultivating new baby plants from your mama plant. This can keep your plants going for generations, is relatively easy, and by multiplying your plants you can grow happiness too! Being in the company of more plants makes us healthier, and sharing your propagations connects us to each other, nature and – you guessed it – also makes us feel good!

PROPAGATING = HAPPY PLANTS

Propagating is good for your houseplants. Plants want to grow, survive and thrive. By taking cuttings and separating out your growing plants you are allowing nutrients, room and light to reach all parts of the plant. Overcrowding can cause plants to compete for light and nutrients – propagating can help the plants to develop and have room to grow to their fullest potential.

PROPAGATING = HAPPY YOU

Research shows the amazing and real benefits that plants can have on our moods. Touching, tending to and handling plants boosts our health mentally and physically. Propagating is no different and aids relaxation, calms our minds and slows us down in a mindful way. It lessens stress and anxiety while boosting positivity and gives you fresh oxygen when you are cultivating more greenery. 'To plant a garden is to believe in tomorrow' is a popular greenie quote. Propagating a small indoor garden has the same optimistic effect – watching something grow, form and develop can give you a sense of achievement and satisfaction.

PROPAGATING = HAPPY WALLET

Raising new plant babies from your existing plants instead of buying new ones can save you tons of money and get you more bang for your buck. It can also help save your pennies when you gift your greens, as these babies make thoughtful and inexpensive gifts for all occasions. I like to bring a baby plant over as a thank-you gift when someone hosts – a bottle of wine doesn't even last the night, but a plant leaves a long-lasting impression and is a kind way to say thanks.

PROPAGATING =
HAPPY RECEIVERS

Giving green gifts that keep growing to family, friends, neighbours or colleagues is a thoughtful and meaningful way to share your love of plants or to say 'hi' or 'thanks'. We all know that sharing is caring and a little cutting or a baby plant from your mama plant shares the wealth. You could also share your little propagated pots of positivity by putting a box of the plant babies outside your home or work with a note to give one to someone who needs a 'plant pick-me-up'. This is a lovely way to share kindness with your community and a planty way to pay it forward.

PROPAGATING =
HAPPY PLANET

Research shows the amazing benefits that plants can have. It's simple: more plants and greenery increase oxygen, life and absorb more pollution and carbon dioxide. Happy days!

WAYS TO
PROPAGATE
GO FORTH AND MULTIPLY!

DIVIDE AND CONQUER

Plants with many branches or stems can benefit from being divided, where you separate off a part of the plant from the top of the branch or stem down to its roots. Water the plant first to soften the soil and allow the water to fully drain out. Remove the plant from the pot, then, using your fingers, carefully tease apart the roots and branches to see where the plant can separate easily into sections. You can choose to divide your plant into two or three parts depending on the size of your pots and space. If the roots are mature and strong you might need to break them up with a spade, stick or tool. Then take the new plant and pot it up carefully with soil – and *voila*! You have a new plant! I recommend giving it a little water to settle the plant into its new pot and home. The ideal time to divide is spring so they have more time to bounce back during the summer growing period.

GREAT FOR DIVIDING

Cheese Plant, Monkey Mask Monstera, Pancake Plant, Brazilian Butterflies, Peace Lily, Sansevierias

chlorine and chemicals evaporate. Change the water about once a week and choose small containers – don't fill them with too much water as this can dilute the plant's natural growth hormone. It's good to use transparent containers so you can see when the roots are formed enough to pot into soil, ideally about 10cm (4in) of roots. This can take two to six weeks depending on the plant, and can be a great way to upcyc\ watch your glass displays begin to root and kids love taking part in this propagating too.

With many of these plants you can also put a cutting directly into moist soil – then keep the soil more on the moist side over the first few weeks so it can take root. You can also buy rooting hormone – you dip the end of your cutting into it before potting and this speeds up the process.

CUTTINGS

In spring to summer, use a clean pair of scissors or knife to take a stem cutting, ideally no less than 10cm (4in) long and cut just a little below a node – this looks like a bump or almost an elbow on a plant stem where new leaves and roots can form. Remove any lower leaves from your cutting then put it into water and keep it out of direct sun. Ideally use filtered water or leave tap water out overnight so that the

GREAT FOR CUTTING

Jade Plant, Pothos, Philodendrons, Begonias, Cheese Plant, Rhipsalis, Wandering Jew, Pancake Plant

PUPS OR OFFSETS

One of the easiest ways to propagate is when a plant creates 'offset' additions. When you see new baby plants, aka 'pups', developing from your plant, you can carefully remove them and pot them up. The ideal time to propagate offsets is spring so they have time to establish roots during the summer growing period. Before removing, make sure the pup is established enough to survive on its own – wait until it is about 5cm (2in) in size or when you dig underneath slightly you see it has roots separate from the mama plant, even if there are just one or two. Gently pull it away from the parent plant or use a sharp clean knife to cut the pup off. Fill a small pot with moist soil, dig a small hole and pop the pup's bottom into it. Keep pups in a bright, but indirectly lit, spot and after a couple of weeks roots will grow and secure in the soil.

GREAT FOR PUPS

Haworthias, Aloes, Spider Plant, Succulents, Pancake Plant

HYDROPONICS

Hydroponic plants are plants that can live and grow in water indefinitely. I've also had luck keeping Cheese Plants and Pancake Plants in water long term, but below is a list of my fave houseplants that can stay in water so you can enjoy them in a glass display – Pothos in particular can make great green foliage for aquariums. Hydroponic plants can help clean the air effectively by removing pollutants – even more efficiently than potted plants as the air can flow faster and in bigger quantities than in compacted soil. Several herbs can grow well in water, such as mint, sage and rosemary.

GREAT FOR HYDROPONICS

Peace Lily, Pothos, Chinese Evergreens, Philodendrons, Spider Plant

CUTTING CLUBS

A fun way to increase your plant collection, save a few pennies and connect with other plant enthusiasts is to start your own cutting club. This way you can share the love with plant-loving colleagues, friends, family or within the community for a different take on plant swaps or seed swaps. It's a great way to meet new plant lovers locally and you might find some already established clubs on social media, however you can easily start your own – we are rooting for you! Sorry again, I had to.

GROWING IN A WINDOWLESS ROOM

TIPS FOR SHADY PLACES

Many of us have a windowless space or room where we would love to add a planty pick-me-up or some greenery either for the wellbeing benefits or for the aesthetics. Here are a few of my tips and tricks to get around spaces that do not offer any or very low natural light.

- **ARTIFICIAL LIGHT** – grow lights with full spectrum light, or bulbs that mimic natural sunlight, can help houseplants to survive in low-lit or light-free spaces. Fluorescent tubes can be a good option as they produce less heat and are low cost. LED lamps can offer light for plants – place them in the specific planty spots, or try LED lights that clip or stick on to surfaces. LEDs are more expensive, but cheaper to run as they are more energy efficient. Grow lights will include guidance for usage, but they want to be placed about 23cm (9in) away from plants and kept on for about 18 hours. Be wary and experiment with 'sun-like' bulbs to make sure that any heat they give off isn't so close that they burn plants.

- **FAUX PLANTS** – there isn't anything wrong with a faux plant for practical reasons, although you will miss out on all the health and wellbeing benefits. However, if it's just for aesthetics, adding fake plants can still create a relaxing and atmospheric green Zen-den vibe to your space.

- **SWAPSIES** – place a low light-tolerant plant in the windowless or minimally lit spot and put it on a plant rotation. Every few days move the low light-tolerant plant into a brighter spot temporarily, or my fave trick is to have another low light-tolerant plant in a brighter spot that you swap about twice a week. See pages 18-27 for low light-tolerant plants.

- **HARDCORE PLANTS** – Peace Lilies have a great reputation for being able to survive in windowless bathrooms due to their ability to deal with the low light and humidity.

POTHOS VS. PHILODENDRON

SPOT THE DIFFERENCE

This is a common mix-up and we can see why. In addition to these trailing vines looking very similar, the common names for Pothos and Philodendron varieties are used interchangeably, for example 'Silver Philodendrons' and 'Satin Pothos' are two names used to describe the same plant. This plant is neither a Philodendron nor a Pothos – it's actually a *Scindapsus pictus*, and though it's in the same family as both of these, it is a different plant. To follow are some simple ways to tell the differences between Pothos, aka *Epipremnum*, and trailing Philodendrons.

LEAVES

'Sweetheart' is a nickname for trailing Philodendrons for a reason: they have a soft-heart-shaped leaf with a thin texture that dramatically curves inwards where the leaf meets the stem. The Pothos leaf straightens as it meets the stem and the leaves are generally large, thicker, broader and glossy.

CATAPHYLL

Heart-shaped Philodendrons grow new leaves from a protective thin casing called a cataphyll. Once trailing Philodendrons' new leaves form and unfurl, these sheaths dry up and eventually fall off. So if you see these papery thin remnants then it's not a Pothos.

AERIAL ROOTS

As they are keen climbers and trail, they both have aerial roots, however Pothos only have one aerial root on their nodes, while Heart-leaf Philodendrons have multiple aerial roots from the same node.

CHAPTER 3

PLANT PROJECTS

Bring plant life into your daily life with this collection of simple botanical-based ideas for practical and mindful uses – a combination of some of my own projects alongside those from friends of Hi Cacti. These DIY projects, crafts and upcycles are great ways to enjoy getting your hands dirty, to consciously connect with nature and bring botanical wellbeing into your life.

POTHOS

HOMEMADE PLANT FEEDS

PLANTS TO FEED YOUR PLANTS

Both of these feeds work well on your plants – and can be made with common household items and ingredients. Being creative and resourceful is one of our greatest gifts. I hope this encourages you to think of other ways to add a sustainable touch to your day to day.

DIY ALOE PLANT FEED

This magical powerful plant will help fuel your other plants because Aloe leaves can be used for a nutrient-rich, all-natural organic plant fertilizer. Just like us, plants will thrive, bloom and grow to their fullest potential when they are nurtured and given the right fuel.

WHAT YOU NEED:

• 2 aloe leaves

• 3.5 litres (6 pints) filtered water (ideally, but tap water can be used)

• Blender

METHOD:

1) Remove the leaves from the bottom of your Aloe as those are the older, more mature leaves and it's less obvious when you've lost them.

2) Cut the whole leaf, including the skin, into large 7-cm (3-in) chunks. Add about a ¼ cup of this fresh Aloe to a blender with 500ml (18fl oz) of the filtered water. Note: this foams up quite a bit, so bear this in mind if you have a small blender. You can freeze any Aloe leaf leftovers for your next fertilizer batch or for use on sunburns or dry skin.

3) Dilute the blended mix with the remaining 3 litres (5¼ pints) of filtered water then – hey presto! – it's ready for you to water indoor or outdoor plants as a natural feed. Use immediately as it can't be stored – it can ferment and start to lose some of the benefits after about 20 minutes of being exposed to air.

BANANA SKIN
LIQUID PLANT FEED

These simple tricks are a great way to use organic banana skin to feed your indoor or outdoor plants. Planet Earth – she provides, she restores and she inspires. Being mindful of how we use our food waste is going to keep her gorgeous and green. You've not only made use of a banana skin that would have otherwise gone to waste, you've also avoided buying pre-made feed in plastic packaging that would eventually end up in landfill.

This simple recipe will turn that banana skin into a powerful potassium liquid feed, which slowly releases nitrogen, phosphorus and magnesium into your soil for happy plants. Potassium protects plants against diseases, strengthens them, helps them to flower and improves the quality of their fruits, nuts or other by-products. See page 78 to learn more about how to fertilize your plants.

WHAT YOU NEED:

- 1 banana skin (preferably organic)
- 1 litre (1¾ pint) water
- A reusable mason jar or clean recycled glass jar with lid

SUPER–SIMPLE METHOD

Cut up banana skin and bury the pieces about 5–7cm (2–3in) away from your plant's stem. Alternatively, lay a banana skin in between the soil layers when you are repotting a plant.

METHOD:

1) Add one organic banana skin to a reusable mason jar or a clean recycled glass jar with a lid.

2) Fill the jar with the water and seal with the lid.

3) Allow to sit for 48 hours or up to one week and then use your natural and homemade potassium-rich drink to help your plants flourish.

MAKE YOUR OWN MOSS POLE

HELP YOUR PLANT STAND PROUD

If you have a Cheese Plant or other houseplant that is starting to lean and could use a little crutch, then fear not – a moss pole is the tool! You can also use a moss pole to help trailing plants such as Heart-leaf Philodendron or Pothos to wind their way upwards. Moss poles can be expensive or it can be difficult to find the size you need, however, this little green-fingered DIY will help you and your plants stand tall.

WHAT YOU NEED:

- Natural lining large enough to wrap around your pole twice – use sheet moss or coco coir/coconut liner for lining hanging baskets or troughs
- Pole – a bamboo stick or PVC pipe
- Twine or string

DO YOU NEED A MOSS POLE?

Sometimes we too need a little extra support, especially during times of change – these are the times of our biggest growth. Who or what can be your 'moss pole'? Is it a friend you can call when you have a wobble of self-doubt, a colleague you can ask for help with your workload when you feel weighed down, or a relative's comfort that can uplift you? Are there people, places or activities that can help build you up when you are feeling 'wonky' like a houseplant? Take a moment to reflect on a person, event or activity in your life that has helped hold you up as you've grown. If you can tell them in a note or phone call then do so – sharing gratitude has a powerful impact on yourself and others. If you can't reach out, then just hold your hand over your heart, close your eyes and thank them out loud. Ask for help when you need it so you too don't become a top-heavy Cheese Plant.

METHOD:

1) Select a pole long enough to go about halfway down your pot. Measure the depth of your pot and then mark this on your pole – this will tell you where to start wrapping the sheet moss or coconut liner.

2) Place your sheet moss or coconut liner down and lay your pole on top – the section marked with the pot depth should lie outside the lining area. Fold down any excess coco lining at the top, then roll the lining tightly to wrap it around the pole, making sure the excess is tucked in tightly.

3) Cut a long length of string (enough to wrap around the pole twice). Wrap it around where your lining starts at the bottom of the pole and tie a double knot to hold the lining in place tightly.

4) Wrap the string upwards and around your pole at a slight angle every 10cm (4in) until you reach the top. Go back on yourself, wrapping the string downwards so it overlaps and criss-crosses over the previous string wraps.

5) Once the string is wrapped back down to the end of the liner or sheet moss, secure the string in a double knot around the base to finish. Then add it to your plant pot – use natural twine to attach the aerial roots or tie additional branches or vines to the string on your moss pole.

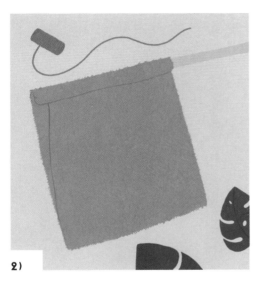

2)

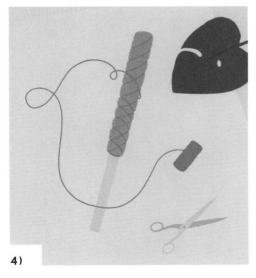

4)

MACRAMÉ PLANT HANGER
CREATE A VERTICAL INDOOR GARDEN

'Get knotty' and create these beautiful bohemian plant pot hangers for a dynamic display of hanging greenery. Textile artist Amy Hepburn lovingly makes our colourful macrame hangers by hand at Hi Cacti and has kindly shared this tutorial so you can make your own. The instructions below make a cute small hanger that will fit a plant or pot that is roughly 8-9cm (3-3½ in). To make a bigger version see page 95. The satisfaction you get when you take time to create something can fill you with a sense of achievement. Self-care can come in many forms, but learning a new skill or trying your hand at it not only gives you a feeling of validation, it also gives you a level of appreciation for how things are created.

WHAT YOU NEED:

- S-hook and horizontal bar or dowel
- 1 wooden or metal macramé hoop
- 6 x 2m (7ft) cotton cord rope (3-ply, twisted or braided), colour or plain
- 2 x 30cm (12in) cotton cord rope (3-ply, twisted or braided)
- Scissors (handle with care)
- Macramé brush or comb

KNOTS:

- Square knot
- Alternating square knot
- Loop knot

METHOD:

1) Take the S-hook and hook it onto your dowel. Add the wooden macramé hoop onto the S-hook. Gather all six of your 2m (7ft) macramé cord lengths, then fold the cords in half over the hoop. Loop one of your 30cm (12in) macramé cords around the six cords going from the bottom of the hoop. Continue until they're held together. Loop downwards until the cord is wrapped around the gathered cord (to a length of 7cm/3in), then tie a knot at the end of the loop to secure the cords.

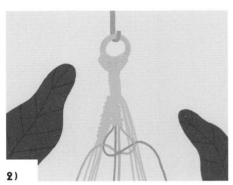

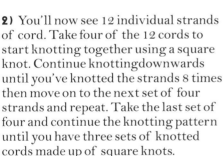

2)

3)

2) You'll now see 12 individual strands of cord. Take four of the 12 cords to start knotting together using a square knot. Continue knottingdownwards until you've knotted the strands 8 times then move on to the next set of four strands and repeat. Take the last set of four and continue the knotting pattern until you have three sets of knotted cords made up of square knots.

3) Take a middle and outer strand from one knotted cord (it doesn't matter if you start from left or right), then another two strands from one of the other knotted cords (if starting with the right middle and outer cords, take the left outer and middle cords) and square knot together. Repeat this formation, going around each of the cords and alternating each row – this is called an alternating square knot.

4) Once you've created 2–3 rows (add more rows depending on the size of the plant and pot), use your other 30cm (12in) cord strand to secure the hanger at the bottom of the final alternating square knot pattern. Repeat the same loop you made for the top of the plant hanger in step 1 until you've looped downwards around the rest of the gathered cord to a length of 7cm (3in). Trim the excess cord and comb or brush out the fibres so the bottom tassels are fringed.

GO BIG – if you need a bigger hanger, add an additional knot to steps 2 and 4 which will make the pot holder 1cm (½in) larger.

MAKE A KOKEDAMA

LITTLE BALLS OF NATURE

Kokedama is a Japanese bonsai technique – kokedama literally means 'moss ball' – and, ladies and gentlemen, that is exactly what you are going to make. This is a wonderful, relaxing and mindful way to bring the outdoors in by creating your own little green sphere of nature and enjoying the process of getting down and dirty at the same time. Creating these whimsical mini green-string gardens is simple and they make beautiful displays or gifts. You will need to mist the moss of your kokedama every few days so that it doesn't dry out. To water the plant just sit the moss ball in a bowl of water for about five minutes once a week. The quantities here should make one kokedama however, if you want to make more, use the soil mix ratio 1 part clay, 8 parts soil, 1 part water.

WHAT YOU NEED:

- 2 tbsp horticultural clay – or alternatively pottery clay or kaolin clay
- 2 cups regular potting soil with perlite for aeration and drainage
- 2 tbsp water
- Plant of choice
- Bucket
- Large mixing bowl
- Sheet moss – approximately 45cm² (18in²), depending on plant size)
- Ball of string or twine: preferably jute twine, but clear fishing line, metal floral wire, hemp cord or waxed cotton cord can be used

METHOD:

1) Place the clay, potting soil and water into a bucket, then mix well and evenly. The consistency can range with variations in soils, clay types and materials. If it is too dry or crumbly, add a little bit more water. If it is not holding together when you try and mould it, then add a little more clay. If it is too muddy, add a little more soil.

2) Remove your plant from its pot, shake off any excess soil and then mould the soil clinging to the roots into a loose ball shape with your hands.

3) Place your plant in a large mixing bowl then take your moist kokedama soil mix and pack a layer around the plant's roots to roughly make a ball shape. You want this to be slightly compact but not too tight, so the roots have aeration – some cracks in the ball are okay. A little hack if you are struggling to get the ball shape to hold together is to wrap sthe soil ball with a thin cheesecloth to hold its shape.

4) Arrange enough sheet moss to cover the size of your kokedama ball – it should be about 2.5cm (1in) thick so the ball will have full coverage and not have holes or thin patches.

5) Place the kokedama ball in the middle of the sheet moss. Wrap the moss around and up towards the base of your plant so it is fully covered up to where the plant stems meet the soil.

6) Take some string and wrap it around the neck of your kokedama once to secure the moss ball. Wrap more string around and overlapping the ball at different angles until the kokedama feels solid and can be handled with the moss staying formed.

7) Once you are happy with the string coverage and it feels secure, tie it off into a knot so it doesn't unwind. You can enjoy your kokedama stationary by sitting it on a dish, drip tray or decorative plate. Or if you would like to hang it then just attach a length of string to the neck of the ball and '*voila*' – your own vertical garden! Enjoy!

FORAGING MOSS

You might be able to forage or gather your own moss in a garden, on private land with permission or from a public path. Collecting this yourself for your plant crafts can be a beautiful and mindful hands-on way to connect to nature. However, only take what you need and do so in a responsible manner as it is part of a sensitive ecosystem and might be protected. You can source sheet moss or sphagnum moss at most garden centres, florists or online.

SUCCULENT WREATH

A SUCCULENT SENSATION TO USE ALL YEAR

This natural dried succulent wreath makes a unique door decoration for any time of year or season depending how you choose to decorate, and embellish it. Your succulent wreath can be made to welcome in the spring or to deck your halls with some house-plant joy at Christmas with wintry dried berries and ribbon! I designed this DIY many years ago and have been teaching this as a workshop since 2016 after I found most succulent wreath DIYs involve decapitating succulents and pinning or hot-gluing them to wreaths, which seemed so wasteful. This decoration is made with live succulents planted into the wreath so you can repot them afterwards to enjoy for the rest of the year, then the dried wreath can be packed away to use again and again, making this craft non-perishable and eco-friendly! This craft in particular allows you to connect to the botanical world and to nature as almost every single material ingredient is natural.

MINDFUL MOSS

Moss is my favourite material in this project and usually becomes everyone else's by the end of the class. It is an ancient plant because it's a survivor – appearing about 350 million years ago in fact. In the depths of winter in some of the coldest places on the planet, when everything else dies, moss will be the only greenery still standing during the cold. Moss can even dry out and then go into a dormant state for years, but as soon as it is rehydrated it will return to life, turn green and lush, and start to grow again. When you next see or handle moss, take a moment to reflect on these miniature forests, how ancient they are and how their thin and fine blankets help release oxygen into the air just like the trees that tower above them. Let the survival of moss resonate for a minute and cast some thoughts on how you too have had to bounce back from certain experiences.

WHAT YOU NEED:

• 5 small succulents ranging from 5.5cm (2in)–8cm (3¼in) pot sizes (add more if you choose)
• Scissors
• Clingfilm
• Jute garden twine
• Natural dried woven wreath base: grapevine, rattan, marilia, moss ring – size optional, but minimum 8cm (3¼in) diameter
• Gardening secateurs
• Moss (either sustainably foraged or bought)
• Floristry pins

OPTIONAL EXTRAS TO DECORATE:

• Cut fresh ivy
• Dried or fresh thistles
• Decorative ribbons
• Dried flowers or dried berries
• Fresh or dried eucalyptus
• Spray paints
• Baubles

METHOD:

1) Before starting this project, water the succulents by giving the soil a good spray. Allow them to dry slightly before using, you do not want the soil to be wet.

2) Squeeze one of the plastic pots to remove the succulent and soil easily. Cut a square of clingfilm big enough to wrap around the roots and soil of your succulent. Put the succulent in the middle of the square, wrap it up and tie twine around the film to secure it to the succulent so the soil is all wrapped up. Repeat for all succulents.

3) To pot the succulents into the wreath base, arrange them on top of the base to decide on their placement. I tend to add the plants and decorations to one section of the wreath to create a cluster effect covering about one-third to one-half of the wreath, but spread the decorations as little or as much as you like.

4) Using secateurs, cut a hole in the front of the wreath base where you want the succulent to go, just big enough for the clingfilmed soil to be potted into. Once in, cut down any excess film that may be showing. Take pinches of moss and tuck them in and around the sides of the hole to surround the succulent; this hides the hole and helps secure the succulent tightly into place. Continue with the other succulents.

5) Once the succulents are potted, start adding any other decorations you want by weaving or sticking them in between the structural weave of the wreath or use floristry pins to tack decorations that need it in place. You can continue to stick in and add as much moss as you please to decorate your wreath or to help hold decorations in place.

6) If desired, spray paint can be carefully used (wearing gloves and a mask) to paint any dried or fresh foliage such as ivy or eucalyptus – make sure the paint is dry before you add this to your wreath.

7) Once the wreath is decorated, use twine or a ribbon to hang your wreath. The succulents can live in the wreath indoors or outdoors for about one month (if there is excessive frost, bring the wreath inside). Then remove and untie the film from the succulents and repot and water them. They can live and be enjoyed until the next wreath.

SUCCULENT WREATH

BOTANICAL BUNDLES
FEEL GOOD AND FRAGRANT

BOTANICAL INSPIRATIONS FOR YOUR BUNDLES

ROSEMARY to energize, awaken, clear the mind and stimulate the imagination.

EUCALYPTUS or **MINT** to feel fresh, breathe easy, revitalize and awaken the senses.

LAVENDER to soothe, calm and relax – a floral lullaby for you and your muscles.

SAGE to ground, detoxify, balance and purify.

AROMATIC SHOWER BUNDLE

This adds an extra touch of relaxation to your downtime – easing stress and anxiety, soothing muscles, and it has added skin benefits too. The herbs will activate when they interact with the heat and steam from your shower to release healing scents that will transform and infuse your self-care.

WHAT YOU NEED:

• Botanical herb of choice

• Garden twine or string

METHOD:

1) Gather a bundle of your favourite aromatic fresh botanicals (see box for inspiration) and tie the ends together.

2) Hold the bundle in the palm of your hand and give it a few gentle taps to activate the aromas.

3) Hang it behind your shower head so it's not directly in the water stream. Breathe deeply and enjoy the sensory experience and relaxation that adding the aromatic plants can bring to your shower routine.

DRYING LAVENDER

Lavender is the perfect scent for sleep and relaxation, so add a vase of dried or fresh lavender to your bedside table or a sachet of dried lavender under your pillow to sing you to sleep with a floral lullaby. For a spot of soothing self-care, add dried lavender to a bath to help decrease stress, promote a good night's sleep, and make your skin smell and feel lush. Additional feel-good ingredients that will enhance your lavender bath soak are 2 tablespoons of oatmeal or a cup of Epsom salts or Himalayan salt to soothe sore muscles.

WHAT YOU NEED:

- Fresh lavender stems (15 max per bundle)
- Gardening secateurs or scissors
- Garden twine or string

METHOD: TRADITIONAL

1) When it's in flower, cut the lavender at the base of the stem with secateurs or scissors.

2) Gather your lavender stems into a small bundle of no more than 15 stems as this can alter drying speed. Tie the base of the stems with twine or string, leaving a long end to use for hanging them up.

3) Leave the bundle in a cool, dry place away from sunlight (this can bleach the colour). Check it every few days, but it should be ready after about one week.

METHOD: SPEEDY OVEN HACK

1) Preheat the oven to its lowest setting (around 50°C/120°F).

2) Spread the lavender stems out on an ungreased baking sheet and place in the middle of the oven.

3) Enjoy the gorgeous smell of the drying lavender stems, but check them every five minutes to make sure they don't burn – lavender is dry once the leaves crumble easily, usually after 10–15 minutes. If the leaves are still moist, turn the lavender over and pop back in the oven for another five minutes. Leave to cool before using.

SIMPLE ALOE LOTION

SUPER-SIMPLE AND SOOTHING

With only three simple ingredients you can make your own all-natural moisturizing lotion. The Aloe cools, soothes, heals, offers pain relief and is antibacterial and anti-inflammatory. This is sensitive enough to be used as a face cream, body lotion, to soothe children's skin, or as an aftersun lotion to treat sunburn or for other burns or minor skin irritations. You can keep this lotion super simple or jazz it up with some essential oils to add scent, extra skin benefits and to relax your body and mind.

WHAT YOU NEED:

- 120ml (4fl oz) Aloe gel – use fresh leaves from the bottom of your Aloe plant or store-bought Aloe gel (ideally all-natural 99 per cent Aloe)
- 40ml (1½fl oz) coconut oil
- 1½ tbsp shea butter
- 5–10 drops of essential oil of choice (optional)
- Mixing bowl
- Whisk, mixer or blender
- Mason jar or sealable storage vessel

METHOD:

1) If using store-bought Aloe gel, skip to step 2. If foraging from your Aloe plants, cut older leaves from the bottom of your plant using a clean knife or scissors. On a cutting board, cut open along the leaf length and scrape out the gel with a small metal spoon.

2) Combine all the ingredients in a bowl and either whisk or blend. Whip so that the shea butter and coconut oil blend to a smooth, thick, creamy consistency.

3) Add the whipped lotion to a mason jar with a lid or a sealable vessel. Put in the fridge for extra longevity and to enhance the cooling and soothing effect, which feels amazing on sunburn. The lotion lasts two years at room temperature or up to five years if refrigerated – just keep the jar sealed and out of the sun or away from heat.

DIY BOTANICAL BATH SALTS

UNWIND AND CONNECT TO NATURE

There is nothing better than a blossom-filled salty soak to work its magic on the body and mind. This super-simple DIY combines a few of Mother Nature's tonics to add some physical and mental benefits to relax your body and mind.

Taking a warm bath for at least 15 minutes with these added ingredients eases stress and even removes toxins from your body, leaving you physically and mentally healthier.

WHAT YOU NEED:

- 1 ¼ cups Epsom salts
- ¾ cup Himalayan pink salt (coarse or fine)
- 1 tsp each dried flowers of your preference (rosebuds, rose petals, chamomile, lavender – see page 103 for drying techniques if using fresh)
- 1 tbsp carrier oil, such as vitamin E, jojoba oil, almond, olive or rosehip oil
- 10–15 drops of essential oil of choice (lavender, rose, geranium, chamomile)
- Medium mixing bowl
- Small measuring jug or mixing bowl
- Reusable mason jar or recycled glass jar with lid

METHOD:

1) Stir together both salts in the medium mixing bowl. Then add the dried flowers and stir them through the mix.

2) In the jug or small bowl, combine the oils and blend together well.

3) Pour the blended oils into the salt mix and stir to cover evenly but gently. Then store in your jar until use. When using you can add half this mix directly into the bathtub while the hot water is running, or if you prefer, pop the salts into reusable muslin cotton bags.

CHAPTER 4

PLANT EATS & DRINKS

Learn how to prepare and eat cactus and other plant-based treats in creative ways while minimizing waste. The recipes for this selection of plant-based treats have been shared by my Mexican friends and our botanical friends. We all believe in respecting and learning from plants and are passionate about promoting sustainable methods, cooking seasonally and buying straight from the source or locally, where possible.

HOW TO EAT CACTUS
PRICKLY PLANT-BASED TREATS

The first time I ever heard of eating cactus I was on a trip with my best friend Lol to Casa Azul, Mexico, to the home of my childhood hero and artist Frida Kahlo. We first spent a sunny day floating down the canals in Xochimilco on a kitsch and brightly decorated gondola-like boat that looked more like a parade float than a mode of transport, and became absorbed into the colours and vibrance of Mexico.

ALL ABOUT NOPAL

We drank cold Carta Blanca beer and chatted in Spanish with our boat driver who was our kind river tour guide. As we passed a bank stunningly lined with cacti, I told him that I had a cactus business in England. He beamed, then proudly described to us how in Mexico they eat *nopalitos* or *nopal*, which comes from the word *nōchtli* in Nahuatl, the language of the Aztecs, and describes the paddles (paddle-shaped leaves) of the Prickly Pear Cactus (aka Paddle Cactus). And the deliciously pretty and pink Prickly Pear Cactus fruit is known as *atún*, translating to 'tuna' in English. Being raised in Texas I was familiar with prickly pear fruits being used in jams and margaritas, but had never heard of eating the cactus itself. Our guide kindly offered to show us how to prepare cactus to cook and eat. I felt like I was living out my own modern-day Frida realness and after that I ate cactus at every opportunity for the rest of our trip. Now I'm a cactus-eating convert.

HEALTH BENEFITS

Turns out nopal isn't just an iconic symbol of Mexico and its people, it's also a healthy superfood. Research continues to reveal its health benefits: reducing inflammation; lowering cholesterol; strengthening the cardiovascular system, intestines and arteries; fighting cardio diseases and slowing cancer growth. It also decreases blood-sugar levels for diabetics and is rich in antioxidants, fibres, vitamins and minerals.

For those with a sweeter tooth, the prickly pear fruit has many of the same benefits – it is uniquely high in vitamins C and D, and contains a powerful neuro-protecting compound. It can be made into juices, purées, jams, salsas and other drinks and dishes. *Opuntia* is the botanical name for the Prickly Pear Cactus genus and there are over 200 species. They all bear fruit, although not all are the edible pears, but most prickly pear fruits on the market are harvested from the Indian Fig Opuntia.

SOURCING AND PREPARING NOPAL

For some, sourcing nopal can be as easy as going for a hike or having some growing in the garden. However, for the rest of us, fresh nopal can be found at some speciality Mexican markets, and jarred nopal (usually preserved in brine) can be found at organic food shops or online (sometimes already sliced or diced). If you get the opportunity to prepare nopal by hand, I highly recommend the experience. For those of you who live in a southwestern terrain scattered with Prickly Pear Cacti, this is how you can prepare your fresh nopal.

1) Cut off the nopal pads and scrub them with a potato peeler to remove all spines and spine nodules. It is normal for the cactus to release some of its slimy liquid, so rinse this off and pat it dry with a paper towel.

2) Brush both sides of the nopal pads sparingly with olive oil and season lightly with salt, pepper and paprika.

3) Grill for about 5–6 minutes on each side till slightly charred. Traditionally this would be done over a wood fire or charcoal, but your oven grill or a BBQ works too.

BOTANICAL DRINKS
REFRESHING AND HYDRATING DRINKS

PRICKLY PEAR DESERT SHRUB DRINK

This desert shrub drink is hydrating, naturally rich in vitamins and minerals, and the apple cider vinegar is great for digestive issues – a 'shrub' is a fruit-based syrup drink mixed with vinegar. Our friend Monique Carr (right) founded Spellbound Syrups, where she creates delicious artisanal beverages from produce foraged in the desert. Here she shares her very own recipe for this botanical elixir. I met Monique in Albuquerque, New Mexico, and was in awe of the fusion of Native American and Mexican cultures there, but also of the connection that my friends and other locals feel to the desert and landscape; something that is clearly at the heart of Monique's business.

For those of us who aren't lucky enough to live in climates where prickly pear fruits can be foraged, speciality food markets usually sell them harvested from September to December. Monique uses a gas stove to singe the glochids (the spiky spines) off before peeling them with a potato peeler. She says:

'Shrubs are the original soft drink before refrigeration: the sugar, acidity and yeast keep the liquid from spoiling and you can use shrub for soft drinks, cocktails, dressings or to pour over ice cream or yogurt. Get creative, have fun!'

WHAT YOU NEED:

MAKES APPROX. 500ML (18FL OZ)

- 6 medium-sized (400g/14oz) prickly pears
- 200g (7oz) raw cane sugar, maple syrup or agave
- 50ml (2fl oz) spring or filtered water
- 40ml (1½fl oz) raw apple cider vinegar

METHOD:

1) Once peeled, cut the fruit into 5cm (2in) pieces and place them into a blender with half the amount of sugar and the water. Pulse until frothy.

2) Strain the blended mix through a fine mesh strainer and cheesecloth into a clean bowl.

3) Add the rest of the sugar and the raw apple cider vinegar and stir until the sugar is dissolved. You can store it in a clean mason jar in the fridge for up to a year.

SIMPLE HIBISCUS TEA (HOT OR ICED)

Hibiscus is a beautiful flower that my mother grows in her garden in Texas and it makes a gorgeous ingredient. Hibiscus flowers are used as a popular fruity flavour or addition to beverages and dishes in the Southwest and Americas. They are packed with beneficial nutrients and high amounts of vitamin C and can help alleviate high blood pressure, menstrual cramps, depression, digestive problems and more. This tasty tea recipe is sweet and fruity but balanced with a hint of sour, which makes it refreshing and hydrating. It can be made from fresh or dried hibiscus flowers – it is very satisfying to watch it brew into a pinky-purple steep. You can enjoy this beverage either hot or iced. You can also incorporate the relaxing and grounding Tea Meditation on page 112 to connect to this recipe and its plants even more.

WHAT YOU NEED:

- 1 mug of boiled water
- 1g dried or 4g fresh hibiscus flowers
- Agave syrup (or honey) to sweeten to your taste
- Lime or lemon – a slice or few drops to taste

METHOD:

1) Boil water and pour into a mug, then add the hibiscus flowers directly into the mug or in a reusable tea bag or tea strainer.

2) Stir in the optional agave syrup, lemon or lime and let the tea brew for about 8–10 minutes.

3) Remove the hibiscus flowers and use them for compost or keep to reuse for the Hibiscus Tacos (see page 124) or syrup recipe (see page 125).

To make iced tea, follow the same instructions and refrigerate to allow the tea to cool after it's brewed – or just add some ice cubes to enjoy sooner.

TEA MEDITATION
CONNECT WITH YOUR SELF AND YOUR PLANTS

A relaxing way to add some mindful meditation to your day and connect with plant life can start with your cup of tea. Tea and herb meditations, in an array of forms, are an ancient means of connecting with the self and with plants. They offer a wonderful way for you to go inwards and breathe into a peaceful flow, while exploring the different qualities and personalities of plants. We are able to connect to their unique complexities through the simple act of a mindful herbal tea tasting. Our friend Sarah McCunn practises herbalism in Brighton and shared with us this little introduction to sensory tea tasting, so go put the kettle on and let's get started.

PREPARATION

You do not need to pick an exotic herb. In fact, it's a wonderful idea to work with a herb you already know well, such as chamomile or peppermint. Prepare yourself a pot or cafetiere of loose herb tea, or you can happily use herbal tea bags, which I recommend doubling up and allowing to steep for 15 minutes.

It's helpful to work with a white cup or mug so that you can see the colours of the tea fully.

MEDITATE AND TASTE

- Find a quiet, comfortable space where you can be for half an hour. Stretch, breathe, yawn and ground yourself into presence.

- Pour yourself a cup of the tea and observe the liquid before you. Tilt it, swoosh it. What colour or colours are presenting themselves? What is the texture of the liquid? Does it appear velvety, viscous or perhaps oily?

- Next, inhale the vapours. How do they interact with your senses? Are there memories or associations that come up? Can you identify different aromas? Perhaps a number of scents reveal themselves.

- Now taste the tea. Roll it around your mouth and tongue before you swallow it. How does it feel? Does it taste as you expected from the smell? Observe any sensations, connections or mental images that arise, positive or negative.

- When you swallow the tea, how does it feel as it enters your body? Can you feel it flow all the way down to your stomach or does it seem to dissolve into your throat or heart area instead?

- When it feels right, sit and breathe in stillness, noticing any subtle changes in your physical or emotional state. Perhaps there is a subtle calmness or groundedness that manifests, or maybe you feel energized or perceive a swirling of movement in a part of your body?

- If the herb you've worked with were a piece of music, how would it sound? If it were a landscape or weather, how would that look? Using what has come up for you, could a character for the herb come forth, human or otherwise?

- Maybe make note of any ideas or thoughts that arise. By immersing yourself in the characteristics of this plant and how those impact you, you are taking a thoughtful step toward deepening your relationship with the plant world and sharpening your senses and imagination. A magical botanical world awaits for you to explore and connect to!

MARGARITAS
COOL CACTUS COCKTAILS

CLASSIC MARGARITA

This recipe pays homage to the Queen of the Desert – the Agave. Agave is the big, bad and beautiful plant mothership from which tequila is derived as well as the agave nectar that we will use to sweeten our super succulent-based cocktail, the margarita! Tequila is harvested from the piña or heart of the Agave, which is then roasted and pressed to make a clear sugary liquid that is fermented and distilled to make tequila. Coming from Texas, this is a staple happy-hour special and *mi favorito* – I would frequently enjoy a cold pitcher with friends at patio bars across Austin, all claiming that theirs is 'the best marg in town'. To make this a flavoured margarita, add 25ml (1 fl oz) of hibiscus syrup (see pg. 125).

WHAT YOU NEED:
MAKES 1 COCKTAIL
• 40ml (1½fl oz) tequila blanco: good quality 100% agave tequila
• 20ml (¾fl oz) freshly squeezed lime juice
• 20ml (¾fl oz) Cointreau or orange curacao
• 5ml–10ml (1–2 tsp) agave nectar syrup (or sugar syrup to taste, see recipe opposite)
• 75g (2½oz) ice cubes or crushed ice

OPTIONAL TO GARNISH
• Sea salt flakes or Himalayan pink salt
• Slice of lime
• Thin slice of fresh jalapeño
• Orange or lime zest

METHOD:
1) Combine all the liquid ingredients with the ice in a cocktail shaker or mason jar with a lid and give it a shake.

2) Optional, but highly recommended, is to garnish by rubbing one of the juiced limes along the rim of the glass to wet, and then dip the rim edge into a small dish of salt flakes. Then add a thin slice of lime to float on top of the cocktail and/or the slice of jalapeno for a little kick. For zesty taste and colour, grate some orange or lime zest an hour or so before to dry, then mix into the dish of salt garnish.

MANGO MEZCAL MARGARITA

A special collaboration with our amigos at Tlaloc Mexican Cuisine, this botanical cocktail elevates a mango margarita by using the earthy smokiness of mezcal to balance the juicy and sweet. Mezcal is similar to tequila in that they are both produced in Mexico and derived from the Agave, but they differ in how they are produced, the regions they are produced in and their flavours. Even though you can replicate this drink with pre-made mango purée, we highly recommend following Chef Corrales' recipe. This allows you not only to utilize all parts of the fruit, but to consider the Agave plant, where it comes from and your ingredients. Handling the fruit, skin and pulp will connect you to the source while creating this sweet and smoky treat.

DRIED MANGO SKIN GARNISH

Take the reserved skins and scrape out the excess pulp using a knife. Cut every skin in three pieces lengthways. Place the skins on a tray, completely cover them with sugar and let them rest at room temperature for at least a couple of hours to slightly dry.

WHAT YOU NEED:
MAKES 1 COCKTAIL

- 3 ripe mangoes (recommended varieties: Manila, Carabao or Philippines)
- Juice of 1 lime
- 200g (7oz) caster sugar
- 40ml (1½fl oz) mezcal
- 20ml (3 tsp) Cointreau or orange curacao
- 7–10ml (1–2 tsp) agave nectar syrup (or sugar syrup to taste)
- 75g (2½oz) ice cubes or crushed ice

OPTIONAL TO GARNISH
- Sea salt flakes or Himalayan pink salt
- Granulated sugar
- Dried mango skin

METHOD:

1) Scoop out the mango pulp, reserving the skins for a garnish. Blend the pulp with half of the lime juice until smooth. This can be made up to two days in advance and stored in the fridge.

2) Combine all the liquid ingredients with the ice in a cocktail shaker or mason jar with a lid and give it a shake.

3) To garnish, rub one of the juiced limes along the glass rim and dip the edge in a small dish of equal quantities of granulated sugar and salt flakes. Add some pieces of dried mango skin to the glass to float on top of the cocktail.

AVOCADO CREAM
A DELICIOUS DEVOURABLE DIP

For the love of the avocado, this fresh and simple treat can be enjoyed on its own as a dip with tortilla chips, or you can use it to add some flair to a salad or your favourite tacos. Chef Daniel Corrales of Tlaloc Mexican Cuisine in Brighton hails from Guadalajara, Mexico, and shared this recipe over an insightful conversation about the importance of being thoughtful about ingredients. He described how working with and familiarizing yourself with seasonal herbs is a great and mindful practice within cooking. It is best to use herbs within their season as they will be at the peak of their quality and flavour. He also promoted using herbs in their entirety when possible – the stems are just as flavourful as the leaves.

WHAT YOU NEED:
SERVES 4 AS A DIP SNACK
- 2 ripe avocados
- Juice of 1 ½ limes
- Pinch of salt
- 1 tbsp chopped seasonal herbs of your choice (coriander, mint, basil or chives)
- Add up to 1 jalapeño if you want to spice this up (optional)

METHOD:

1) Cut each avocado in half lengthways around the seed with a knife – be careful not to damage the stone if you want to use it later for growing (see opposite). Twist the halves to open, gently remove the stone with a spoon and set this aside. Scoop out the avocado flesh.

2) Add the avocado, lime juice, salt, herbs and jalapeño (if using) to a blender or processor. Blend until smooth (around two minutes). Taste and add more salt or herbs if needed.

3) Pop the avocado stone you reserved into the middle of the dip as a fun garnish – the stone also prevents the avocado dip from discolouring if you are preparing in advance. For best results, consume fresh the same day.

GROW YOUR OWN AVOCADO PLANT

This process of sprouting avocado plants can be a great way to teach kids about growing plants. Your new avocado plant will thrive in bright, indirect light, and needs watering when the soil feels dry to the touch – about 5cm (2in) deep. The circle of life can continue in your kitchen!

WHAT YOU NEED:

- 1 avocado stone (cleaned)
- 4 wooden toothpicks
- Glass jar

METHOD:

1) With the avocado stone tip pointing upwards, stick four wooden toothpicks evenly around the middle, about halfway down – a minimum of 5mm (¼in) deep – like compass points. These will hold your stone securely in place.

2) Place it on the rim of the jar, so the toothpicks suspend the stone tip. Fill the jar with water so the bottom of the stone sits in the water. Keep topping up the water level as needed and leave in a warm spot with indirect sun.

3) After four to six weeks roots should start to form. Once the roots reach about 10cm (4in) and reveal a couple of leaves, remove the toothpicks and pot the stone halfway up in all-purpose soil.

PLASTIC BOTTLE METHOD

You can replicate the same method using a recycled plastic bottle. Cut off the top of the bottle just where the neck begins to taper. Turn the cut-off top upside down and place it back into the bottle so the stone can suspend and sprout this way without the toothpicks.

AVOCADO CREAM

CACTUS CONDIMENTS

DELICIOUS DESERT TREATS

PRICKLY PEAR & RED ONION CHUTNEY

I met the ladies of Planted vegan catering at the early stages of us all starting our plant-inspired businesses. We bonded through supporting each other, sharing ideas and experiences, and organizing special events themed around our mutual passion and ethical approach to working with plants. Gabriella, the co-owner, and I bonded early over our love of prickly pears, so her unique and alternative way to create this chutney was the perfect recipe to share. This chutney is lovely served with bread or in addition to a sandwich, to be paired with vegan cheeses and crackers or used as a dip.

WHAT YOU NEED:

MAKES AROUND TWO 300G (11OZ) JARS OF CHUTNEY

- 16 prickly pear fruits
- 500g (1lb 2oz) red onion (sliced)
- 125g (4½oz) golden caster sugar
- 75ml (2½fl oz) white wine vinegar
- 1 cinnamon stick (or ½ tsp ground cinnamon)
- A grating of fresh ginger (or dash of ground ginger)
- Big pinch of salt

METHOD:

1) Set aside 3–4 prickly pears. Prepare the rest by slicing each in half and scooping out the middle – compost or discard the skins. Place the scooped-out flesh in a saucepan and cook down until it has turned into a liquid mush. Strain it through a sieve, making sure you push all the bits through apart from the seeds.

2) In a saucepan on a medium heat, add the sliced onion, sugar, vinegar, cinnamon, ginger, salt and sieved prickly pear. While this is heating, peel and roughly chop the 3–4 prickly pears you saved from earlier and add them to the pan. Bring to a boil then simmer for an hour or two, until thickened. Spoon the mixture into sterilized jars and seal with a lid.

3) Once the jars are cooled, store in a cool place. Once opened, refrigerate and consume within one month but for best results, consume fresh the same day.

SALSA CON CACTUS

This tasty chunky mix is my jazzed-up, colourful version of a traditional pico de gallo, a classic Mexican salsa-like salad. Back home in Texas almost everywhere you go for drinks or a meal you would be greeted and seated with a bowl of complimentary pico de gallo or salsa and tortilla chips at the table as a little welcoming tradition, so this is my usual BBQ or party offering when I'm a guest. This savoury mix adds beautiful and fresh flavours when used in burritos or tacos and is a crowd pleaser when served as a salsa dip with tortilla chips.

WHAT YOU NEED:

SERVES 4

- 70g (2½oz) nopal cactus pads or strips (fresh or jarred)
- 5 tomatoes – roughly 300g (11oz) – chopped into 2cm/¾in chunks
- 1 red onion (finely chopped)
- 5 slices pickled jalapeno, or finely chopped fresh jalapeno for more heat
- 2 garlic cloves (crushed)
- Small bunch of coriander, roughly chopped (including stems)
- 70g (2½oz) corn kernel pieces
- Freshly squeezed juice of 1 lime
- ½ tbsp freshly squeezed orange juice
- Salt and freshly ground black pepper

METHOD:

1) If using fresh nopal, follow the instructions for preparation on page 109 and allow to cool before using. If preparing from jarred nopal in brine, rinse the pads and then lay them in between paper towels to dry. Cut the nopal into 2cm (¾in) chunks and place in a mixing bowl.

2) Add the rest of the ingredients, mixing well, and season to taste with a big pinch of salt and pepper and more lime juice. Leave to rest in the fridge for 20 minutes, to give the flavours a chance to develop and marinate before you eat. Bring to room temperature before serving.

CACTUS CONDIMENTS

BLOOM WHERE YOU ARE PLANTED.

CACTUS TACOS

ALL DAY LONG

In my hometown, we eat tacos for breakfast, and having 'hot sauce in your bag' isn't just a Beyoncé lyric. Breakfast tacos are commonplace all over Mexico and the American Southwest, and they vary in style and ingredients – but breakfast tacos in Austin are a serious business! Whether it's from a roadside taco stand, a taco trailer, cafe or restaurant, you can expect a killer taco – you can be queuing for hours to get one and it's still worth it. I usually rustle up a big batch of my taco filling on a Saturday morning so we can reheat to enjoy over the weekend or share with friends. You can make these tacos without the cactus if you are struggling to source it, but adding it gives this dish loads of extra health benefits so I recommend trying it at some point. Quick and easy, this little plant-based 'all-day taco' recipe is my adaptation of a taste of home.

WHAT YOU NEED:
SERVES 4

- 100g (4oz) nopal cactus pads or strips (fresh or jarred)
- ½ tbsp rapeseed oil or sunflower oil
- 2 x 300g (11oz) tins of peeled potatoes (approx. 360g (12½oz) once drained)
- 170g (6oz) corn kernels pieces
- 1 x 400g (14oz) tin of black beans (approx. 250g/9oz once rinsed and drained)
- ½ vegetable stock pot
- 1½ tbsp ground cumin
- 1 tsp paprika powder, plus extra for sprinkling
- ½ tsp garlic powder (optional)
- 1 tsp liquid smoke (or soy or tamari)
- 1 tsp your favourite hot sauce (or more to taste for extra kick)
- Tortillas of your choice
- Salt and freshly ground black pepper

METHOD:

1) If preparing fresh nopal, see the instructions on page 109 and then follow from step 2. If using jarred nopal in brine, rinse the pads and then lay them in between paper towels to dry. In a frying pan over a medium heat (with no oil), season lightly with salt, pepper and a sprinkle of paprika. Heat on each side for about three minutes until slightly brown or charred. Take the nopal off the heat and set aside.

2) In a large pan, heat the oil on a medium heat and when hot add the potatoes, corn kernels, black beans, vegetable stock, cumin, paprika, garlic powder (if using) and liquid smoke. Cook for about 8–10 minutes, stirring occasionally to combine the seasoning and ingredients.

3) Cut the nopal into 2cm (¾in) pieces and stir into the taco mix. Season with salt or hot sauce to taste.

4) Serve on warm tortillas with vegan sour cream, salsa or some avocado. You can mix in scrambled tofu or scrambled egg before you serve, if you choose. Now y'all enjoy your plant-based Tex-Mex tacos and consume within five days.

GUACAMOLE (OPTIONAL)

For avocado lovers, you can follow the recipe on page 116 for Avocado Cream or make this simple guacamole to garnish.

WHAT YOU NEED:

- 1 ripe avocado
- ⅛ tsp fresh lime juice
- Balsamic vinegar
- 1 small red onion, finely chopped
- Salt and freshly ground black pepper

METHOD:

1) Mash the avocado, lime juice and a couple of drops of balsamic vinegar with a fork. Mix in a little red onion and season to taste.

CACTUS TACOS

123

HIBISCUS TACOS

TASTY PLANT-POWERED TREATS

This recipe is a favourite of mine from the creatives of Tlaloc Mexican Cuisine. These amigos have helped cure my homesick Mexican palate while sharing some truly inspired dishes with a welcoming *'mi casa es su casa'* culture and sustainable ethos. The hibiscus flowers in this dish could be those left over from preparing the Hibiscus Tea (see page 111) – a great way to minimize food waste. This will inspire you to add creative and sustainable practices to your own kitchen.

WHAT YOU NEED:

SERVES 3

- 150ml (5fl oz) sugar
- 300ml (10fl oz) water
- 250g (9oz) dried hibiscus flowers
- 1 large garlic clove
- ½ white onion
- 1 guajillo chilli (or any other chilli)
- 25ml (1fl oz) soy sauce (or use tamari sauce for a gluten-free option)
- 4 corn tortillas
- Rapeseed oil or sunflower oil
- Fresh ground black pepper

TO GARNISH

- Pico de gallo (see page 119)
- Avocado Cream (see page 116)
- Red onion, finely sliced
- Fresh coriander, finely chopped
- Fresh lime

PLANT EATS & DRINKS

METHOD:

1) Dissolve the sugar in a pot with the water and bring it to the boil. When the water starts to bubble, add the flowers and cook for five minutes. Then drain the flowers of excess liquid – when cooled, this can be used as a syrup to add to sparkling water or to a margarita (see page 114).

2) Finely chop the garlic and onion and slice the chilli in half, discarding only the stem.

3) Heat the oil in a frying pan over a medium-high heat. Once the oil is hot, add the chilli halves and fry for around two minutes. When the chilli is fried, remove from the oil (if you like extra spice, scrape out the chilli seeds into the pan and discard the chilli). Turn the heat down to medium-low and add the chopped garlic, stirring constantly until golden brown.

4) Add the chopped onion and keep stirring until it is translucent. Add about 2 tablespoons more oil to the pan and once heated add the flowers, stirring constantly to fry them evenly for about two minutes. Then add ground black pepper to taste and the soy sauce (or tamari sauce) to cook, stirring constantly for another two minutes or until caramelized, then remove the pan from the heat.

5) Heat the tortillas in a comal or a large pan and once they are warm, serve them filled with the avocado cream, flower filling, red onion, pico de gallo, coriander and squeeze some fresh lime on top.

CHAPTER 5

PLANT DESIGN

Choosing the right houseplants for your space is only part of the fun! Once you bring your new green housemates home you get to play around by adding your own style and taste to your plant life. So get creative with these clever, fun ways to display your plants and help them settle into their new home.

WATERMELON PEPEROMIA

PLANT POTS

PICKING A POT FOR YOUR GREENS

Selecting the perfect pot can be an enjoyable and playful way to set off a plant and make it come alive, literally. Choosing a pot for your plants allows you to tie together colour palettes, textures, patterns, materials or themes in your space. For example, if you have marble counters in your bathroom you could source marble-effect pots as a nod to the décor, or liven up a sterile or beige office space with colourful or patterned pots. When selecting pot materials, bear in mind that plants will thrive in containers that help them mimic their natural conditions. Here is some inspiration and information to consider when choosing indoor plant pots.

PLASTIC

If you have thirstier plants that thrive in a slightly more moist environment, such as Peace Lilies, Cheese Plants and Pancake Plants, plastic pots could be helpful homes as they enable the soil to retain its moisture for longer.

CLAY OR TERRACOTTA

Houseplants from hot or dry climates do well in terracotta or clay pots as they are porous and replicate their stony and rocky terrains with clay in the soil. Cacti and succulents suit clay pots as, if overwatered, the pots can soak up some of the excess moisture and slowly release it into the soil. If you're not into traditional terracotta pots there are many styles and shapes to choose from. You can get other colours, such as grey or white terracotta pots, which offer a slightly more modern and sleek look.

comes to watering this isn't ideal for the container's longevity as with time the water will warp or destroy the wood.

GLASS

Planting directly into beautiful glass globes, bottles or containers can make for beautiful terrariums and displays. However, many plants do not fare well in these containers as the glass retains moisture and limits the air flow. In these environments moisture-loving plants such as Polka Dot Plants, Nerve Plants, mosses and some ferns work well, but layers of drainage are needed between the soil and glass to avoid mould and root rot.

Some plants can be propagated in water and some plants are hydroponic, meaning they can live in water indefinitely, such as Pothos – see more suggestions on pages 85. Watching plants grow in water and seeing their entwined roots makes for an otherworldly and mesmerizingly interesting point of view.

Select unique clear or coloured glass containers to create a water-based but beautiful alternative indoor garden display. These could be old test tubes, chemistry-style beakers, vintage crystal decanters, recycled jam jars and bottles, antique mason jars, your favourite spirit bottles, interesting fish tanks or fish bowls, you name it!

CONCRETE

Concrete pots are also porous, so if you pot a houseplant that requires regular watering directly into a concrete pot, you may have to increase the frequency or volume of water to compensate for the thirsty pot. Plants such as *Sansevierias*, ZZ Plants, succulents or cacti do well in concrete containers.

WOOD

Plants that grow in or off tree trunks in their natural habitat do well being grown off wooden mounts, such as Staghorn Ferns, air plants and some others. As for wooden pots or wooden frames for regular plants, if you want to create this look and effect you can line the wooden containers with plastic sheets or pond lining. However, when it

PLANT POTS

129

PEACOCKING PLANTS

If you have a patterned or colourful plant, consider a minimal, plain pot or something neutral like a concrete pot to let the plant do the talking.

CANNED CACTI

Tin cans can also make inventive and inexpensive vessels for your plants. You can treasure hunt at antique or junk shops to find interesting vintage tins or upcycle some of your favourite tea, biscuit or sauce tins. I love using leftover hot sauce tins for my baby cacti, adding a touch of the American Southwest to my kitchen windowsill in England. Clean the tin out well first and create drainage holes by hammering a nail into the bottom of the tin. Add a heavy layer of gravel or pebbles at the bottom before you add soil and pot the plant.

FINAL THOUGHTS ON VESSEL MATERIALS

Choosing the right pot material for your plants will help you play to your strengths or weaknesses with watering. If you are someone who overwaters plants, keeping them in more porous pots like concrete or clay will compensate for your overloving tendencies. Or if you tend to forget to water your plants, then plastic pots will help them retain moisture in between your forgetful bouts of watering.

DRAINAGE

No matter what type of pot you use, most plants survive and thrive with good drainage. When you water a plant, the soil wants to get a drink, but any excess water should be able to flow through the soil so the plant's roots don't saturate and drown due to lack of airflow. A typical dilemma for most house-plant fans is sourcing indoor plant pots with drainage holes. Usually the only pots with drainage holes are the plastic nursery pots that plants are sold in or standard outdoor terracotta pots. So I hate to break it to you, but the adorable little succulents you see in fun vessels like sweet little teacups aren't too happy about it. They will show you their unhappiness as soon as you water them – the water sits in the bottom of that cute cup with nowhere to go,

giving your succulent root rot. Many of the beautiful and fun indoor plant pots on the market don't have drainage holes either, so here are some hacks that I recommend.

POT WITHIN A POT– does what it says on the tin and this is what I personally do with many, but not all of my plants. I keep my plants potted up in the plastic nursery pots and then sit them inside my lovely (but slightly less functional) indoor plant pots without drainage holes so the plant is encased in a more visually appealing pot. However, when I water the plants I just take the plastic potted plant out of the indoor planter shell and stick it in a sink or tub so the water can flow right through and escape – then I pop it back into the pot.

CREATING DRAINAGE LAYERS – if you have your heart set on potting your plant directly into an indoor pot with no drainage hole, you can add a good layer of stones or pebbles to the bottom of the pot to compensate.

ADD A HOLE – just as it sounds, you can carefully drill a hole at the bottom of a pot – use a tile drill piece to drill through ceramics. If it's a metal or cute vintage tin you can hammer a nail into the bottom a few times to let the water escape.

PLANT SHELFIES

IF YOU'VE GOT IT, FLAUNT IT

Now that you've picked the plant and the pot you get to enjoy the final touch of nesting with your houseplants – displaying your plants. Less can be more of course and simplifying your space is a great idea, unless you're more of a 'go big or go home' than minimalist chic kind of person.

GREEN UP YOUR LIFE

Adding a few greens to your bookcase, top shelves, fireplace and desk space is going to relax your brain when you are in that space, increase your productivity and boost your mood. Keeping plants and caring for them gives us a daily connection to nature and a satisfying sense of purpose. Inspiring and eye-catching 'shelfies' can be a shelf, worktop, bookcase, fireplace or desk space arranged with houseplants as a form of self-expression. Nesting and adding greenery within a space makes it feel more personal and welcoming for you and others around you.

FILL THE VOID

Homes and offices have little nooks and crannies where some visually pleasing greenery can fill the boring and barren! Adding a tall, thin freestanding plant, such as a ZZ, into a slightly shadier spot is a great way to disguise a naked corner without taking up too much floor space. Or you can use a leafy plant like a Cheese Plant as a clever hideaway for plugs, cables or other eyesores like storage containers.

WABI–SABI VS HYGGE

Before the Scandinavian word 'hygge' was used to describe a feeling of cosiness, there was the ancient fifteenth-century aesthetic and philosophy of wabi-sabi. Rooted in Zen Buddhism, wabi-sabi is about embracing a simple, authentic way of life close to nature, and about finding beauty in its flaws. Adding plants to your space immediately adds nature into your daily lifestyle, while adding soft textures to your interiors, which studies show eases our brains, allow us to relax and sleep better. So whether you're feeling a bit more wabi-sabi or cosy hygge, embracing plant life offers us peace, comfort and tranquillity.

PLANT SHELFIES

BUTTERFLY AGAVE

NATURE NEEDS TIME TO BLOOM. SO DO YOU.

The fun doesn't have to end there! When it comes to styling your greenery you can embellish your plants and pots with extras that add a special personal touch to gifts or can inject some fun, creativity and aesthetics to your plant–pot combo.

POT STICKS

Sticking a decoration into the pot soil can be an interesting addition. You can find or make some beautiful pot sticks, adding fun little messages or signs. For kids it's fun to add in a little animal or toy figurine to live in the green jungle. I like adding Mexican milagros, hammered metal charms used for prayer, to some of my plants, which ties in with my Mexican and Southwestern home décor.

TOPPING IT OFF

Topping it off – literally means adding shells, coloured pebbles, gravel, or more to the top of your soil to add some colour, texture or aesthetics. I love adding crushed white shells to the top of my cacti at home as they really set off the cacti. These toppers have added benefits as they can prevent plant soil from staying too moist, especially in winter months. They can also stop mould spores from growing on top of your plant soil, which is beneficial as these moulds can affect your sleep if you have plants in your bedroom.

I wouldn't recommend adding pebbles or shells to top plants that grow new stems or have growth from the roots up as these coverings would restrict them and stunt growth. However, plants such as succulents and cacti come from rocky and dry mixed soils naturally so they like this extra layer of drainage.

CRYSTALS

Another special and magical adornment you can add to your potted plant is a gemstone or crystal. This especially can add some thoughtful meaning when gifting plants to others. Here are a few gemstones that we like to add to our plants to give them a bit of mystical and sentimental meaning.

AMETHYST – gemstone of intuition and healing

CITRINE – gemstone of dreams and manifestation

MALACHITE – gemstone of protection

ROSE QUARTZ – gemstone of love and compassion

SELENITE – gemstone of enlightenment and cleansing

TIGER'S EYE – gemstone of resilience and action

TOURMALINE – gemstone of grounding and protection

STYLING YOUR PLANTS

HANGING GARDENS

GROW UP TO MAXIMIZE YOUR SPACE

For spaces with high ceilings, a high hanging indoor garden can be dramatic and breathtaking. Alternatively, for small compact rooms or spaces where counter space or worktops are limited or already overflowing with plants, this is another way to maximize your available green space! Whether you use indoor hanging pots with luscious, long trailing plants, kokedama planters or boho handmade hangers, nothing says 'jungle at home' more than plants flowing from the sky – okay, ceiling. Plants such as String of Hearts, String of Pearls, trailing Sweetheart Philodendrons, Pothos, Spider Plants or Wandering Jews can drape around your space in their glory.

HOOK UPS

Command hooks and other plant wall hooks can help tidy up big plants to create botanical canopies or green trailing wall displays. Another trick for those who want a wall of green without the cost and care issues is to have a layer of faux trailing greens on the wall and then put the real live hanging plants over the top. This gives a thick, jungle effect, but requires half the care – the bottom plants would struggle to get enough light to give it a dense layer of green and the real plants mask the faux look, so it's not noticeable. And for renters who love the effect but aren't able to make holes or drill into ceilings, a simple 'S' hook hanging off the end of a curtain rail or shower rail can be an easy and accessible way for your plant to hang out.

FINAL THOUGHTS

Nature shows us that where there is a will there's a way. If you look to nature she usually reflects back some pretty awe-inspiring and motivational examples of perseverance.

NATURE SHOWS US HOW TO 'JUST KEEP GROWING'

I was recently driving down the M25, one of the busiest motorways in London, and was floored when I saw a 2m (7ft)-high sunflower in full bloom – despite its unlikely setting in a crack in the concrete of the dual carriageway. How inspiring it is to see Mother Nature's little messages spring up as if to show us how to 'just keep growing'. Tree roots will spread in unlikely shapes and form around roads or obstacles, reflecting to us that even plants and nature can teach us that you can 'grow through what you go through'. Mint, grass or other greenery will emerge from any crack in the pavement to reclaim their wild and survive. One of my favourite pastimes is to seek out, explore and photograph abandoned man-made spaces that are now growing wild again – nature has literally taken back.

A GREENER FUTURE

It's so motivating when you see the creative new ways in which humans are harnessing nature and plant life in sustainable practices for the future. Here are just a few of many plant-powered examples: prickly tall cacti planted to create natural barriers to replace fencing or walls; large, spiky Agaves planted under windows as a natural but spiky deterrent for intruders; cacti used as an alternative to leather products; jojoba berries and other plant oils replacing the use of whale oil in beauty products; and fields of Aloes (being almost completely water) planted in California as a natural defence against the forest fires that contribute to climate change. We can also look back at plant practices and learn insights from our early ancestors who were so connected to nature, and participate in a renaissance of appreciating and utilizing nature's gifts.

GREEN UP YOUR LIFE

Throughout this book we've explored and learnt together how plants really are our allies and insightful teachers – and sometimes even a botanical therapist! Plants really can be the cure, they nourish us inside and out, brighten up our spaces, purify our air, bring us some calm in a sometimes chaotic world, offer a touch of comfort for self-care, add health and love to our meals and help soothe physical ailments.

So get out there and green up your life – it's good for you, the community and the planet. Make some seed bombs and go tackle an urban green space, car park or empty field to beautify your city or hometown; or start growing your own urban garden; or propagate plant babies to share the love and encourage others to go green. Nature reminds us to stand tall and to nurture ourselves and each other – not just to survive but to thrive.

INDEX

BIG THANK YOUS

To my boyfriend, fur baby Otto and houseplants who, in no particular order, bring joy and calm to my life. Just kidding Dan, thank you for being my rock and co-pilot.

Myself and *Hi Cacti* have been inspired and shaped by my hometown of Austin, Texas, so big thanks to my family, amazing friends and Austinites that make it 'weird', warm and wonderful, thanks ATX.

To my sister Roxy and best girlfriends near and far from LA, San Fran, Austin and Brighton, you are ALL my cheerleaders, thanks for always rooting for me! And Lolly you were there from day one on my first market stall – thanks for always believing in me. Miranda, for introducing us to Tucson and its deserts, our spirit home. Amanda who helped fuel my fire early on with your 'girl power'. My first intern Maya Doyle turned friend, turned amazing illustrator of this book. Love ya! Thank you Monica, Caroline and team who helped make this book and dream come true! Thank you to my amazing 'green goddesses', aka the Hi Cacti tribe, and the makers who help make the business a unique botanical haven. Hi Cacti is an independent, female-run and owned business and we owe our growth to our fab customers and community here in Brighton. Thank you!

A MASSIVE thanks to the National Parks, The National Trust and conservation groups for taking care of these earthly wonders, their plants and their animals so that we can venture out and connect with nature.

And to YOU! Thank you for reading this book. Green-fingered or not, WELCOME, y'all are now part of our Hi Cacti community. To connect, use the hashtag #hicactibook to share your plant goals and introduce us to your green roommates – share your photos, hacks, crafts and plant-based self-care there.

CONTRIBUTORS

MONIQUE CARR
SPELLBOUND SYRUPS
@spellbound_syrups

DANIEL CORRALES
TLALOC MEXICAN CUISINE
www.tlalocbrighton.co.uk

AMY HEPBURN
HEPBURN'S CRAFTS
www.etsy.com/shop/hepburnscrafts

SARAH MCCUNN

GABRIELLA RIZZELLO
WE ARE PLANTED
www.weareplanted.com

LOL SWIFT
LOL SWIFT COACHING
www.lolswiftcoaching.com

PHOTOGRAPHERS

XAVIER BUENDIA
xdbphotography.com

EMMA CROMAN
emmacroman.com

DAN LADD
@isoyounothing

KENNY MCCRACKEN
kennymccracken.com